THE COMPLETE GUIDE TO BERNEDOODLES

Cover photo courtesy of:
Ruth Sommers - Utahbernedoodles.com

David **Anderson**

TABLE OF CONTENTS

Introduction **6**

CHAPTER 1

What is a Bernedoodle? **8**
Physical Characteristics 11
Behavioral Characteristics 13

CHAPTER 2

Choosing a Bernedoodle **16**
Where Do I Find My Bernedoodle? 16
Adopting a Bernedoodle 17
The Right Breeder 19
Finding the Right Breeder 22
The New Puppy's Health 23
Picking Out Your Puppy 23

CHAPTER 3

Preparing Your Home for Your New Bernedoodle **26**
Preparing Your Children and Pets 26
Household Dangers 29
Preparing a Space for Your Dog 31

CHAPTER 4

Bringing Home your Bernedoodle **34**
The First Day 35
Going to the Vet 36
Pet Supplies 39
The Cost Breakdown 40

CHAPTER 5

How to be a Puppy Parent **42**
Chewing 43
Digging 44
Growling and Barking 45
Separation Anxiety 46
Running Away 48
Bedtime 48

CHAPTER 6

Housetraining **50**
Housetraining Options 51
The First Few Months 52
Positive Reinforcement while Housetraining 53
In the Event of an Accident 54
Crate Training 55
Doggy Doors 56
Housetraining Adult Dogs 56

CHAPTER 7

Socializing your Bernedoodle **58**
Interacting with Other Dogs 59
Socializing Your New Dog with Current Pets 61
Introducing Your Dog to Other People 62
Introducing Children to Your New Bernedoodle 64

CHAPTER 8

Bernedoodles and Your Other Pets **66**
Introducing Your New Puppy 67
Pack Mentality 68
Fighting 70
Raising Multiple Puppies 71
What to Do if Your Pets Don't Get Along 72

CHAPTER 9

Training your Bernedoodle **74**
Getting Everyone on the Same Page 75
Operant Conditioning Basics 76
Primary Reinforcements 77
Secondary Reinforcements 79
The Dangers of Punishment 80
Professional Dog Training 82

CHAPTER 10

Basic Commands **84**
Benefits of Proper Training 84
Basic Commands 85
    Sit 85
    Lie Down 86
    Stay 86
    Come 87
    Off 87
    Drop It 88
    Leash Training 89
Advanced Commands 89
    Fetch 90
    Shake 90
    Take It 90
    Go 90

CHAPTER 11

Nutrition **92**
Importance of a Good Diet 92
Essential Nutrients 93
Adjusting for Different Life Stages 96
Different Types of Commercial Food 96
Homemade Food 97
People Food 98
Obesity and Dieting 100

CHAPTER 12

Grooming Your Bernedoodle **102**
The Bernedoodle Coat 102
Brushing and Bathing 104
Trimming the Nails 106
Brushing the Teeth 107
Cleaning Ears and Eyes 108
Professional Grooming 109

CHAPTER 13

Basic Health Care **110**
Visiting the Vet 110
Preventative Care 112
External Parasites 112
Internal Parasites 114

Supplements and Holistic Treatments 114
Vaccinations 116
Pet Insurance 116

CHAPTER 14
Advanced Bernedoodle Health **118**
Common Ailments in Bernedoodles 119
Common Ailments in Bernese Mountain Dogs 120
Illness and Injury Prevention 122

CHAPTER 15
Travelling with Bernedoodles **124**
Dog Carriers and Restraints 125
Crate Training 126
Car Rides 128
Flying 129
Hotel Stays 130
Kenneling and Dog Sitters 130
Tips and Tricks for Traveling with a Dog 132

CHAPTER 16
Life With an Aging Bernedoodle **134**
Basics of Senior Dog Care 135
Grooming a Senior Dog 136
Nutrition 137
Exercise 138
Mental Stimulation 138
Common Old-Age Ailments 139

INTRODUCTION

Whether you are a proud owner of a Bernedoodle, are considering getting a Bernedoodle, or have never heard of them, this guide will give you a complete look at everything you need to know about this crossbreed. Bernedoodles are a relatively new breed, but once you spend some time with one, you'll understand why they are quickly gaining popularity.

Raising a dog is no easy task—it takes a lot of time, energy, and the commitment to giving your pup the best life possible. But, with a willingness to take the time to learn about a dog's needs and to work hard, you'll be ready for a Bernedoodle in no time.

Bernedoodles, or the cross between a Bernese Mountain Dog and a Poodle, are special dogs. Every breed has little differences that require different types of care and attention. By the end of this book, you'll understand this breed's unique qualities and how to address their needs.

First, we'll take a look at what a Bernedoodle is, in terms of breeding. This first section will describe the physical and behavioral characteristics of the dog. This includes the different coat types, size, and behavioral tendencies. You'll be able to find out if the Bernedoodle is a good fit for your lifestyle.

Next, the book will discuss everything that a prospective Bernedoodle owner needs to know before they bring a new puppy home. While the chapter on breeders and places to adopt Bernedoodles will tell you what you need to know to obtain one of these fluffy pups, there's so much more to know. Subsequent chapters will help you prepare your house, your other pets, and your family for the big day.

After you prepare your household, you need your dog to get off to a good start in life. The following chapters will give you all the information you need to make the first few weeks a breeze. You'll read about socializing your new dog with other people and pets, setting rules and expectations for your dog, and housetraining.

Then, after the new puppy knows its place in the family, it will be ready for obedience training. The section on training covers basic commands, plus a few more advanced tricks. Bernedoodles love to learn, so once they understand your reward system, they'll have a great time learning new commands. In this section, you'll learn the right and wrong way to train a dog, and pick up helpful hints and suggestions along the way.

Finally, the last several chapters deal with the health of your Bernedoodle. As you'll discover, diet and grooming have a major effect on their overall health and wellbeing. Preventative health care will save you and your dog a lot of stress (not to mention money) in the long run. You'll learn about what to feed your dog and how to keep it looking clean and tidy.

From there, you'll learn the basics of veterinary care. Bernedoodles have very specific health issues, but once you know what to look for, getting your dog the right diagnosis will be simple. You'll also learn about all the things you can do in your own home to keep your dog healthy. The final chapter will give you a look into the future at your Bernedoodle in its senior stage of life.

Overall, this book should provide the reader with a basic guide from picking out the perfect Bernedoodle to its final life stage. You'll find that owning a Bernedoodle is a big commitment, but it's worth it. A happy and healthy Bernedoodle will add so much joy to your life. With the information in this book, you'll have all the knowledge you need to raise your newest family member.

Photo Courtesy of Diane Caldemeyer-Reid
www.cortarveterans.com

CHAPTER 1

WHAT IS A BERNEDOODLE?

Photo Courtesy of Cheryl Ziegler

A Bernedoodle, also known as a Bernese Mountain Poo, is a cross between a Bernese Mountain Dog and a Poodle. They are considered to be a "designer breed" because they are the offspring of two purebred parents. In this breed, the best characteristics of both Poodles and Bernese Mountain Dogs are combined to create a one-of-a-kind pet.

Tracing the origin of this breed can be difficult, because it is hard to know where any breed first began. Also, many pups around the world are not necessarily bred for a specific purpose, so there could be many "naturally occurring" mixes. Perhaps one of the first breeders to be recognized for the Bernedoodle is Sherry Rupke of SwissRidge Kennels. Rupke began breeding these dogs in the early 2000s, and they have become exceedingly popular ever since.

Often times, when one breeder introduces a new and exciting crossbreed, other breeders, professional and amateur, recognize a new demand in the market and begin producing their own crosses. Once prospective dog owners see these adorable fluffy dogs, it is hard to resist finding one of their own. From there, the breed becomes more and more popular, until it is recognized by the public. This breed isn't formally recognized by the American Kennel Club, but is accepted by various designer dog organizations.

For the past several decades, Poodle crossbreeds have taken over the market. If you're looking for a fresh take on your favorite breeds, Poodle crosses are a good pick. Along with their virtually no-shed coat, they have certain behavioral characteristics that are valued in a good family pet. When the Bernese Mountain Dog and the Poodle are combined, the result is a mild-mannered dog that loves to play.

As with any crossbreed, there are different ways to make a Bernedoodle. Perhaps the most common is the basic Bernese Mountain Dog-Poodle cross, using two purebred parents. This generation of offspring are half Bernese Mountain Dog and half Poodle and are characterized as F1 Bernedoodles.

From there, there are more variations that breeders use to hone the perfect mix of characteristics from the two pure breeds. Another type of cross is done with a Bernedoodle and a Poodle. The resulting offspring have a curlier coat that doesn't shed as much as the first generation Bernedoodle, and are referred to as F1B Bernedoodles. Some breeders may even breed in a variation of the Poodle, like the Bernedoodle, or the Miniature Poodle.

Finally, depending on what traits breeders want displayed in their dogs, they may cross an F1 Bernedoodle with another F1 Bernedoodle, an F1 with an F1B, or even two F1B Bernedoodles. While the first generation Bernedoodles, or F1 Bernedoodles are typically known for their good genetic health, breeding cross breeds with the same cross breeds results in greater consistency in physical and behavioral characteristics.

To understand the characteristics of the Bernedoodle, it helps to know more about their parent breeds: the Bernese Mountain Dog and the Poodle.

Bernese Mountain Dogs originated as Swiss working dogs that were capable of pulling carts and herding livestock. These big, strong dogs were perfect for hauling heavy loads for Swiss farmers. Once modern technology replaced the need to work, they became companion dogs for owners who loved their sweet disposition.

As with many working breeds, the Bernese Mountain Dog is capable of learning and enjoys having a job. This dog is smart and is easily trained. It is a gentle breed, making it a good family pet. Bernese Mountain Dogs are sensitive creatures, so a firm, yet gentle hand must be used with training, as to not discourage them from learning. Because they are slow to mature, Bernese Mountain Dogs remain in their "puppy stage" for longer than other breeds.

This is a giant breed that is capable of weighing about a hundred pounds. They have a distinctive brown, black, and white multicolored coat. This breed's top coat is long and silky and their bottom coat is thick and wooly. Because of their coat type, they shed a lot, which can be a problem for some owners.

Photo Courtesy of Tanis Connors

The downside to this beautiful breed is that they have a short lifespan. Due to their size and genetic makeup, this breed only lives between six to eight years on average. This breed is susceptible to many genetic diseases that may cause life-ending illnesses. Their short lifespan is often a deterrent for dog owners looking for a new member of their family.

Bernese Mountain Dogs do best in cool climates where they have ample room to run around and play. Strenuous exercise in warm conditions can cause this furry breed to overheat and become ill. This breed needs room to roam, so apartments and small homes don't fit this dog's needs. Access to a yard is necessary for Bernese Mountain Dogs to get the exercise they require.

The Poodle is a popular dog in breeding because its coat type and behavioral characteristics enhance other breeds. It's not certain where this breed originated because there are so many ancient dog breeds that it is similar to. Regardless of its origin, the Poodle as we know it today is an old breed that was a good worker. The Poodle was used for hunting waterfowl, sniffing truffles, and even performing in circuses.

This is one of the most intelligent dog breeds, so training Poodles is a breeze. They are smart and eager to learn new tricks. While Poodles often have a snooty reputation, they are actually loyal, friendly dogs that get along well with people. They can be silly and playful, but also focused and obedient when necessary.

The Standard Poodle is not a small dog by any means. They can weigh around 50-60 pounds, with males typically a bit larger than the females. This breed also features the smaller Miniature size, and the even smaller Toy size. These size differences are useful for creating Poodle crossbreeds of different sizes.

Perhaps the biggest draw to owning a Poodle is their distinctive coat. While no dog is entirely hypoallergenic or shed-free, the Poodle's coat and saliva do not trigger a significant allergenic response in most people. They shed an almost undetectable amount of fur, making them great indoor pets. Their curly coats come in a wide variety of colors. Unfortunately, this breed requires a lot of grooming to keep them looking good.

This breed can live in a variety of different homes, but still requires a fair amount of exercise. If Poodles have too much energy and nowhere to expend it, then they may become bored and destructive. A long walk or a game of catch can keep their minds and bodies happy. As opposed to the Bernese Mountain Dog, Poodles have a much longer life span of twelve to fifteen years.

Physical Characteristics

The Bernedoodle is the best of both worlds: a big, snuggly dog with a coat that doesn't shed excessively. This crossbreed can inherit different characteristics from its parents, so there is a wide possibility of behavioral and physical traits that you can get. For this reason, it's important for breeders to use the right Bernese Mountain Dogs and Poodles when creating a cross. If you understand what the parents are like, there's a good chance the Bernedoodle will be just like them.

While there is a lot of variation with this crossbreed, there are some characteristics that are pretty common across the board. The more these dogs are bred, the more consistency there is in coat type and behavior. While there are some outliers, you'll find that most Bernedoodles are a happy medium between the two breeds described above.

Like its parents, this is a giant dog. On average, the Standard Bernedoodle grows to twenty six inches and eighty pounds. Because the Bernese Mountain Dog can also be crossed with different sizes of Poodles, it is possible to breed a Miniature Bernedoodle and a Toy Bernedoodle. The Miniature Bernedoodle grows to twenty inches and forty pounds, and the Toy Bernedoodle is fifteen inches and anywhere

66 *Bernedoodles come in three different sizes: Standard, Mini/Medium, or Micro-Mini which is great for someone looking for a smaller dog. They also come in a variety of colors ranging from traditional tri-color, bi-color, sable, and even cream."*

Carol Heller
www.highmesadoodles.com

Photo Courtesy of Kara Hamby

Photo Courtesy of Megan Glass
www.glasshousepuppies.com

between ten and twenty four pounds. There is a Bernedoodle of every size, from ten pounds to over a hundred pounds.

Bernedoodles come in several different color combinations. Like the Bernese Mountain Dog, Bernedoodles can be white, black, or brown. However, they may be one solid color, a combination of two colors, or even have the tri-color coat.

One major reason that the Bernese Mountain Dog is crossed with the Poodle is for improved coat texture. Depending on how the breed is crossed, there are three common coat types. The straight coat is perhaps the least common in this cross-breed, because it sheds the most. Wavy coats are much more common. This coat is long and silky. For people who suffer from allergies, this coat may not be enough to keep them from experiencing symptoms because it sheds a moderate amount. The third type is short and curly. This coat is most likely to be found in the offspring of a

Bernedoodle-Poodle cross. The curly coat is similar to that of a Poodle's and is the least likely to shed of the three types.

The curly coated Bernedoodle or the F1B is the best pick for allergy sufferers, because they shed the least. But if the prospective pet owner has serious dog allergies, it is best to do an allergy test with the new litter. Even within the same litter, some pups cause a greater reaction than others. A breeder should provide fur or saliva samples for testing before a purchase is made.

Behavioral Characteristics

With any crossbreed, you can expect the offspring to share the behavioral characteristics of the parent breeds. Like Bernese Mountain Dogs, Bernedoodles have an especially prolonged puppy stage. While their bodies matures quickly, it takes their brains a little longer to catch up. This trait may affect how quickly this breed can be trained in the early stages. Training at a young age is possible, but owners should prepare for a slightly stubborn puppy. Housetraining might take a little more time and effort, but once the puppy outgrows this stage, it won't be an issue. This breed may also be a little more sensitive during this stage, so make sure that training is positive and accidents aren't dealt with harshly.

Bernedoodles are intelligent dogs and they enjoy learning new things. Obedience training is necessary for keeping their behavior in check and keeping them entertained. As the offspring of two working dogs, this dog enjoys having a "job" to do, whether that takes the form of playing a game of fetch or performing fun tricks.

Photo Courtesy of Steve Hetherington

Photo Courtesy of Ariel Leon

An intelligent dog makes training a breeze, but it also means that it gets bored more easily. The best way to deal with boredom is by giving the Bernedoodle plenty of attention. These dogs need plenty of play time with their owners to keep their minds active. If they don't have enough constructive things to do, they may show destructive tendencies. They get lonely easily, so owners must make sure that they have plenty of time to spend with the dog.

Along with a healthy mind, these dogs need plenty of exercise for a healthy body. They have moderate exercise needs, so they cannot be cooped up in a small space for too long. Daily walks are a necessary part of a Bernedoodle's healthy lifestyle and a large, fenced-in backyard is also great for this breed. They are moderately energetic, but that doesn't mean that they don't enjoy a little down time as well.

The Bernedoodle may be shy at first when meeting new people, but will warm up after enough socialization. When it comes to meeting new people, give this breed a little time to sniff the person out. This slightly wary nature makes them decent guard dogs because they are more likely to bark at intruders. They are moderately protective of their people, so they'll be on the lookout for strangers.

Bernedoodles are extremely friendly dogs and give owners lots of love and affection. They are sweet and goofy dogs that will keep their owners entertained, too. These dogs make good family pets because they get along well with children. They are playful but gentle, making them a safe choices around children once they've been properly socialized.

Experienced breeders will breed pups with the best physical and behavioral characteristics. These traits are passed down from generation to generation, so well-behaved parents tend to produce well-behaved offspring. If you're looking for a Bernedoodle that fits specific needs for your home, a good breeder can help you find the right dog.

NAUGHTY

CHAPTER 2

CHOOSING A BERNEDOODLE

Photo Courtesy of Carol Heller
www.highmesadoodles.com

Always do your research before purchasing a new puppy. Weather you choose a Bernedoodle or any other breed you want to make sure that the breed you choose is the right fit for your family. After all you are going to have the dog for the next 10-14 years and you want to make sure that you and the dog will enjoy your lives together."

Carol Heller
www.highmesadoodles.com

Where Do I Find My Bernedoodle?

Once you've decided that the Bernedoodle is the right dog for you, it's time to pick out the perfect pup for your home. When choosing the right dog, there are so many options for where to go.

The first decision to make is whether you want to purchase or adopt. There are pros and cons to each, so it's important to know what you're looking for in a Bernedoodle. Adoption is great because it provides a good home to a dog that might not otherwise have a place to live. Animal shelters across the world are filled with great dogs that just want loving homes. Re-homing fees are usually a lot lower than the cost of buying from a breeder, so adoption is a good choice when you might not have the money to buy.

On the other hand, you don't always know what you're getting with an adopted dog. If you have special preferences for your dog, it may take awhile for the right Bernedoodle to enter a shelter. Dogs that come from a reputable breeder are more predictable than adopted dogs. Before choosing, it's important to explore all of your options.

Adopting a Bernedoodle

Adopting a dog is such a rewarding experience. When you adopt, you may be saving a Bernedoodle from being euthanized if it can no longer be cared for. Once you've decided to bring a Bernedoodle into your home, consider taking some time to look around local shelters and rescues for the right dog. It can make a huge difference in an animal's life.

There are many benefits to adopting that many people do not consider. In most cases, adopted Bernedoodles have lived in a home before. That means that there is a good chance that they've been socialized with people and other animals, and they may know basic commands. If the Bernedoodle spent any time inside, then they are probably already house trained. Training is a challenging and time consuming process, so if you don't have the knowledge or time to train a Bernedoodle, adopting is a good way to find a dog that's ready for your home.

Rescue Bernedoodles will also come with a lot of things already done that owners would have to do for their puppies. Most shelters dogs have undergone a health screening to make sure the dogs are in good shape before being adopted out. They will also have all of their necessary vaccinations and will have been spayed or neutered. Many shelters will also microchip their dogs to ensure that they don't return to a shelter because they got lost.

Photo Courtesy of Tanis Connors

Photo Courtesy of Tanis Connors

There is typically an adoption fee that comes with a new dog, but it is relatively low in comparison to purchasing a Bernedoodle from a breeder. This fee covers the cost of the veterinary care the dog received while in the shelter and other basic costs. Adoption fees are usually less than the amount of money that went into caring for the dog while in the shelter, so you're getting a lot for your money when you adopt.

There are a few downsides to consider when adopting a Bernedoodle as well. Sometimes, a dog's history is unknown. Unless the previous owner gives the dog's behavioral and medical history to the shelter, you might not know what you're getting. In many cases, fantastic dogs are put into shelters because the owner had to move or has passed away. Other times, dogs are put into shelters because of behaviors that were not compatible with the owners. Many behavioral issues can be worked with, but there are some instances where you need to know the dog's behavior before bringing it home. For example, if a dog was put into a shelter because it was aggressive with other pets or children, you may not want to bring that particular dog into your home if you have kids or pets.

If the owner is set on finding a Bernedoodle puppy, it may take a long time before one is available for adoption. You're more likely to find adult dogs in shelters as opposed to puppies. Bernedoodle puppies are irresistibly adorable, so once they become available at shelters, they get adopted quickly. Many prospective dog owners are looking for a pet that will be in the family for their entire life, so senior dogs usually get left behind in shelters.

Finally, it can be challenging to adopt a Bernedoodle unless your home and lifestyle are deemed a good fit by the shelter. Many animal shelters have strict rules for adopting and require home checks. This is done for the dog's best interest so that it won't be returned to the shelter because it wasn't a good fit. There will probably be lots of paperwork to fill out and questions to answer before a dog can enter your home. For Bernedoodles, shelters will look for someone who lives in a home with a fenced-in backyard and active owners who have the time and ability to give their Bernedoodle plenty of exercise.

There are many resources out there to help you find your perfect Bernedoodle. Some websites let people search for specific types of dogs in shelters in the area. Even if your closest shelter doesn't have any Bernedoodles available, there might be a shelter a few towns away with one. Bernedoodle rescues are another good place to check out because they cater specifically to people who want to find the right Bernedoodle. Some rescue organizations also have volunteers who will transport your dog to you if you're unable to make the trip to pick up your Bernedoodle.

As tedious as the adopting process can be, it is absolutely worth it to bring a loving and appreciative Bernedoodle into your home. The adoption process is arranged to ensure that both the dog and the owner are happy. It may take some extra time and effort to find the right Bernedoodle, but it is incredibly rewarding to give a dog a new home.

The Right Breeder

The other option when looking for a Bernedoodle is purchasing directly from a breeder. Buying a Bernedoodle is a good choice if you specifically want a puppy, can afford to spend a lot of money on a dog, or are looking for a very specific type of Bernedoodle.

When you purchase a Bernedoodle from a breeder, there's a good chance that you know how the dog will turn out. Unlike when you adopt a grown dog, when you buy a puppy, you will be training and socializing the dog from scratch. For some owners, this is appealing because you get to enjoy watching your dog grow up and become a well-behaved adult. You'll get to learn the history of your pup's health and their parents' health. You can also be sure that your dog is a true Bernedoodle and not some combination of different breeds.

Because Bernedoodles are often bred for people with dog allergies, a breeder may be the best source of Bernedoodles if you cannot tolerate just any dog. Some dogs are especially bred to lessen the allergic response in humans, so you'll know that you can handle their dander and saliva in your home.

When finding the right breeder for the right Bernedoodle, there are a lot of things to keep in mind. A good breeder is experienced, knowledgeable, and ethical. Bernedoodles are considered "designer dogs" which means that they are not a purebred dog, but a cross between two different pure breeds. Poodle crossbreeds have gained popularity over the past few decades, so it's not hard to find someone who will breed Bernedoodles.

However, not just anyone can and should breed Bernedoodles. Breeding is all about genetics and it's not an easy subject to tackle. It takes the right knowledge of dog breeds and favorable characteristics to make the right crossbreed. A good breeder must choose two healthy parents with known physical and behavioral traits. For example, using a Poodle with aggression problems may lead to aggression in the pups. If a breeder is selling Bernedoodles for people with allergies, they must know how to add other breeds to the cross to make a dog that does not trigger an allergic response.

Good breeding is also extremely important for the health of the Bernedoodle. Both breeds are known for certain conditions that can be passed down from parent to pup. Improper breeding can sometimes result in rare sizes or colors, but it can also wreak havoc on the dog's health, causing health conditions that can shorten a dog's lifespan.

Also, the breeder should be passionate about the breed. A breeder that takes a special interest in Bernedoodles should strive to only produce the best dogs. Often, good breeders will show their dogs in competition because they take pride in their work. They should not be afraid of having experts examine and judge their dogs. Instead, they should want to show off their dogs because they know they've done good work.

An excellent breeder breeds Bernedoodles not for the money, but for the love of the breed. With many newly popular breeds, non-professional breeders will get into the business because they can see how much money they can rake in for producing puppies. People who take advantage of breed popularity are probably not as educated in breeding and passionate as those who devote their lives to it. If you buy from a poor breeder, you may spend a lot of money for a poor product. If you don't take the time to get to know the breeder, there's the danger of being scammed. A good Bernedoodle breeder has been in the business for a long time and has the customer base to back him or her up.

Another good way to find reputable breeders is to visit their facilities. Good breeders will let you come into their homes to see how the dogs are treated. Look for clean, comfortable conditions for the dogs. The dogs should have plenty of room to roam around, inside and out. The area where the dogs live should have fresh water and toys, and be clear of waste. Puppies kept away from people in cramped conditions is a warning sign that the dogs are not properly cared for. Socialization with people and other dogs begins at birth, so they should not be isolated in any way.

Finally, the Bernedoodle breeder should have plenty of contact with the buyer. Good breeders care about their Bernedoodles long after they go to a new home. They will not let a dog leave until it is at least eight weeks old. Breeders should also ask the buyer questions to make sure that they are sending their dogs to a good home. They should not be afraid to speak their opinion if they believe that the buyer is a bad fit for the dog. A good breeder doesn't mind if you visit a few times and take some time to think. After all, adding a new member to the family is a big commitment, so they'll want to make sure you're comfortable with your decision.

After your dog goes home with you, the breeder should keep in contact with you to check in. They should make themselves available for answering questions and giving advice about the breed. If there are any problems with the new home and the owner cannot take care of the dog, the breeder may even take the dog back into their care. Sometimes, a breeder will insist that you have your dog spayed or neutered. This is so their pup doesn't contribute to overpopulation or get used by amateur breeders.

Reputable breeders will be able to answer any questions you have about Bernedoodles and will ask you questions about yourself in return. They will be easy to contact and happy to speak with you. Good breeders are passionate about Bernedoodles and have the client base to back them up.

Photo Courtesy of Cheryl Ziegler

Finding the Right Breeder

Photo Courtesy of Carol Heller
www.highnesedoodles.com

“ *Don't select your puppy based solely on coloring. Make sure you are getting a dog with a personality that matches your lifestyle. A good breeder should be able to help you with this.*”

Megan Glass
www.glasshousepuppies.com

Once you know what makes a breeder good, it's time to find one. First, check out trusted organization websites. Bernedoodle enthusiasts will help you find the best breeder in your area. Also, it's not a bad idea to check out dog shows where Bernedoodles will be competing. There, you'll be able to see the dogs in action and get in contact with the breeder. Vets are also good sources for any kind of dog-related advice. If they have any Bernedoodle clients, they may be able to direct you to them.

Once you have the contact information for a few breeders, it's time to narrow your search. A good breeder might give you the contact information of their clients. Make sure to ask the clients about their Bernedoodle's health and behavior. Look for customers with adult dogs that are in good health and are well-behaved. Some problems in the dogs may not be evident until they are a little older. If you know that the breeder's dogs are healthy into adulthood, you can assume that their current pups are in at least that good of shape.

Visit a few breeders and take a look around their facilities. They should have their credentials and awards on display to show off their successful work. They should not only show you the puppies, but also the parents. If the parents are in good health and are friendly then that's a good indication that their offspring will be, too.

Another thing to consider is the price of the dog. Compare prices and see what services are being included. If you see two similarly priced puppies, see what kind of money has been put into the puppies already. The cost of vaccinations and check-ups can be high, so make sure that the breeder has put that money into the health of the puppy to make sure you're getting your money's worth.

The New Puppy's Health

Like with any product people buy, the buyer needs to make sure that they're getting a high quality puppy. One way to do this is to receive a health certificate from the breeder. Prior to their sale, the breeder should have their pups checked out by a veterinarian. Once they are examined and are deemed to be in good health, the vet issues a health certificate.

Along with the puppy's check-up, the breeder should also be able to provide a full medical history of its parents. It is easier to test adult dogs for a variety of diseases and conditions, so the parents' health is maybe even a larger indicator of the puppy's health. You should not only be able to meet the parents yourself, but also see their health clearances. You should see test results for hip and elbow health, eye health, and other genetic conditions.

Finally, the breeder should provide you with some sort of guarantee contract. They will assure you that the puppy is in good health, but it's also good to have your dog checked out once it's in your possession. This protects both the buyer and seller in case there are any problems with the pup.

Most health guarantees will have different clauses telling the buyer what will happen if their dog is in poor health due to poor breeding. This makes the second check-up necessary. This way, you're sure that the breeder's health screening was legitimate and the breeder has proof that if any illness comes up, it was not due to breeding.

In most cases, if your dog becomes ill due to a genetic condition, the breeder will give the customer a discount to cover the vet bills. Even if you don't expect a discount, it's a good idea to inform your breeder if any problems arise. This way, they know that something went wrong and they can fix it before the next litter comes along.

Picking Out Your Puppy

Once you've picked out the perfect breeder, it's time to pick out the perfect puppy. Bernedoodles can be different colors, so you may be able to choose by your favorite coat color and texture. However, you should not choose by appearance alone—it's important to take behavior into account.

While it may be hard to choose just from a few short minutes with the litter, the breeder knows them best. They have been with the puppies for at least eight weeks, so they know their unique behavior. But if you don't want to take the breeder's word for it, there are a few things you can look out for.

First, see how the puppies interact with one another. If there's one that's aggressive with the others, they might not get along well with another dog. Similarly, if there's one that's especially submissive, they may get picked on by other household pets.

Photo Courtesy of Carol Heller
www.highmesadoodles.com

" Bernedoodles love to be the center of attention! They will put on a show for anyone that will watch. The fun thing about Bernedoodles is that no two are exactly alike in their looks. From Day one they are very distinct in personality and in their appearance."

Diane Caldemeyer-Reid
www.vonfarawayfarms.com

Next, see how they act apart from one another. Puppies should be curious and approach a friendly person. If they bark too much at you or cower in the corner, they might be wary of people. If one seems completely uninterested, they may not be as bright as the others. If they are too energetic or aggressive towards you, then they might be too much for a home with children or other pets.

While these may not be foolproof tactics for choosing the right dog, it's a good way to gauge how these dogs will react around others as adults. More socialization and training will be needed, but some behaviors will stay the same throughout the dog's life. When looking at a range of behaviors in puppies, choose one from the middle. They're the most likely to be friendly and sociable.

Finally, check to make sure the dogs are in good health. If you have a reputable breeder, this shouldn't be necessary, but it's a good idea to check anyway. They should have a round body and not be too skinny. Check the eyes, nose, ears, and mouth for any unusual discharge or crustiness. Watch their gait and note any abnormalities in how the puppies walk or jump. They should also be responsive to noises and be able to track an object with their eyes.

After they are eight weeks old, the puppies are ready to go to their new home. If you pick the right breeder and get your choice of the litter, then you can be sure that you're bringing home your new best friend.

Whether you're adopting or buying from a breeder, make sure you know what you're looking for in a Bernedoodle. Choose a dog that's in good health and displays behaviors compatible with your lifestyle. Talk with the breeder or shelter workers to get as much information on the dog as possible. Once you've made your choice, it's time to bring your Bernedoodle home.

CHAPTER 3

PREPARING YOUR HOME FOR YOUR NEW BERNEDOODLE

" The ideal home is one with lots of love to give. It is always best if there is someone home with the pup, especially through the early stages. They love to get in the car and go as well!"

Diane Caldemeyer-Reid
www.vonfarawayfarms.com

Before bringing your new Bernedoodle home, it's important to have your home prepared for your new family member. Being prepared means that there will be less stress for you and your Bernedoodle. As you get ready for your dog, make sure that your house will comfortable and safe for everyone in your household.

Preparing Your Children and Pets

If you're bringing a new dog into a home with children, then you've already made sure that your Bernedoodle has a good history of being around kids. By nature, Bernedoodles are very gentle, friendly, and protective, which makes them get along well with children. Regardless of their temperament, any dog can be bothered by a child that does not know how to act properly around dogs.

While older children may be more experienced with handling animals, young children need to learn how to treat dogs before the pup comes home. Tell the children that the new dog needs to be treated nicely. This means to approach the dog slowly and pet gently. Young Bernedoodles can be timid, so it's important to take things slow so it doesn't get scared.

Keep in mind that very young children need to be supervised while with your dog. No matter how gentle your dog is around people, it doesn't take much for it

Photo Courtesy of Shelly Perras

to go into defense mode. Dogs will nip at people when they're annoyed or hurt as a warning to back off. It's easy for young children to get comfortable with the dog, but if they get too excited or play rough, there may be negative consequences.

If the Bernedoodle becomes visibly frightened or stressed, give it a few moments alone to calm down. One bad experience with a dog can cause an aversion to dogs, and you don't want your child to be afraid of the pet you've worked so hard to bring into your home. Especially with young children, an adult should always be present while they are interacting with a dog.

If your children don't have a lot of experience with pets, teach them how to properly pet your Bernedoodle. To be safe, show them how to gently pet down the back of the dog. It's best to keep away from the face altogether, because little fingers may poke a tender spot or reach a little too close to sharp teeth.

Once the Bernedoodle feels safe and comfortable with the children, have them participate in obedience training. Show your kids how to say commands to the dog. This will help your dog and your children understand one another. As a bonus, playing a role in pet care is a good way to teach children about responsibility.

If you have other pets, this is the time to prepare them for a new sibling. If your current pets are typically friendly with other animals, then there's a good chance they'll be good to your new Bernedoodle. However, there is no way to predict how your pet will act when a new guy enters the home. Just like with children, your Bernedoodle should be approached slowly and gently by other pets.

First, set up a place in your home for the dogs to meet. Find a room or outdoor space that is free of your dog's belongings. This way, there aren't any personal possessions nearby to feel possessive about. You may consider keeping the dogs on leashes and having a few extra hands available so you can control how quickly they check each other out. Give them time for a few cautious sniffs before letting them free to play.

When bringing a new puppy into the home, it's a good idea to have baby gates on hand. Not only does this help with housetraining, but it's a good tool to use to keep your pets separate if necessary. If you're nervous about how your pets will interact with the new pup, you may want to make a special space for it. Gates will allow your animals to see and sniff one another, but lend a little extra protection for your puppy.

Finally, make a plan with your family members to spend equal amounts of time with each pet. New puppies are exciting, but your older dogs may become resentful of the little one if they aren't getting their fair share of love. If your other dogs feel like they're getting the attention they need, they're less likely to turn on the new puppy.

It will take some time for your Bernedoodle to become comfortable with other people and animals around, but preparing your family for your new arrival will make the process easier and less stressful for everyone involved.

Most animal shelters and breeders will allow home visits before bringing a dog home for good to ensure that the dog is a good fit. While it can be difficult to discover that the Bernedoodle isn't compatible with your current home life, it's best to find this out early. Sometimes, no amount of training or socializing can protect your new Bernedoodle from other pets, and some dogs just don't get along with kids. For everyone's safety, be on the lookout for signs that the new dog just isn't working out.

Household Dangers

If you've ever seen anyone "baby-proof" a home, then you'll understand the process of making your home safe for your new Bernedoodle. Bernedoodles are curious creatures and probably won't always be under your supervision at all hours of the day. It doesn't take long for a dog to sneak away from your watchful eye and get into something it shouldn't. Prevention is key—check your home for hidden dangers before bringing your new dog home.

To a dog, a house looks like a magical place with tons of yummy foods to try. Unfortunately, there are lots of things that can cause a dog to become very ill if ingested. The most obvious place for your dog to get into something dangerous is in the kitchen. While you may not

❝ *You want to puppy proof your home make sure all items you don't want to be chewed on are picked up. Make sure the puppy has plenty of toys of its own to chew on. Don't leave anything lying within their reach that could poison them or make them sick."*

Carol Heller
www.highmesadoodles.com

Photo Courtesy of Ariel Leon

Photo Courtesy of Ariel Leon

think twice about leaving snacks out on your kitchen counter, keep in mind that your Bernedoodle is a big dog, and they're capable of climbing on furniture to get what they want. Some people foods are perfectly harmless to dogs, but some can cause illness and should be stored in cupboards that your dog cannot gain access to.

Chocolate is one of the biggest food dangers. Even a few bites can cause vomiting, seizures, and even death, if not treated immediately. Foods like macadamia nuts and coffee also cause similar reactions in dogs. Fresh produce isn't safe, either. Onions, garlic, grapes, and avocados can all cause organ damage if consumed in sizeable quantities. The popular sweetener xylitol can also make your dog very ill if it eats a baked good or sweet that contains it.

When it comes to people food, it's best to keep all of it away from your Bernedoodle. Instead of worrying about the harmful ingredients in the foods you eat somehow finding their way to your dog, keep everything out of reach. People foods are generally not great for dogs in the first place, so removing any tasty temptations will help keep your Bernedoodle healthy.

After checking the kitchen, take a look around for dangerous houseplants. Popular houseplants like English ivy, lilies, umbrella trees, and dumb cane can all cause symptoms like seizures, vomiting, diarrhea, and gastrointestinal pain. Some plants are perfectly harmless, but it's a good idea to do some research to see if your house plants are dangerous to dogs. Another option is to put your houseplants in hanging baskets or in other hard to reach areas. Also, take a look at the plants in your yard, because common flowers like tulips or daffodils can cause illness if your dog digs up the bulbs and ingests them.

Garages and sheds are filled with all sorts of things that dogs might like to taste. Antifreeze is enticing to dogs because of its sweet smell. However, ingesting even a little will make a dog ill. The same goes for common gardening chemicals like insecticides and rodent poison. Keep these things far away from your Bernedoodle's reach.

Bathrooms and other places where harsh cleaning solvents are found are another dangerous place for dogs. If cleaning products are not safely stored away, a curious Bernedoodle might try to taste it. Keep medications tucked away in a cabinet and out of reach. Also, many dogs like to drink out of the toilet. While this behavior is already pretty gross, consider all of the harsh chemicals used to clean the toilet that are now in the dog's body. Get in the habit of closing the lid after each use.

Finally, never underestimate what your Bernedoodle will try to eat. Small, household objects like socks, coins, and small toys can be choking hazards and can cause bowel obstructions. Cords may look like a nice chew toy, but can cause a nasty shock. When in doubt, remove all items that your dog might try to eat and replace them with vet-approved dog toys to keep them interested.

When it comes to potential dangers in the home, there's no need to panic. Take a few days before you bring your new Bernedoodle home to clean your home and store dangerous plants, chemicals, foods, and miscellaneous items in places that dogs can't reach. Once you bring your Bernedoodle home, if you find that it is particularly crafty, it's a good idea to invest in some child-proof latches and baby gates. With good training, your dog will eventually have a better idea about what is okay to chew and what is off limits.

Preparing a Space for Your Dog

While you may plan to eventually let your Bernedoodle roam freely around the house, it's best to give them a smaller space of their own to start with. Especially with puppies that are prone to accidents, letting your dog move freely will create

66 *Bernedoodles are total klutzes: completely uncoordinated and clumsy. And don't even get me started on their tree trunk sized tails. Nothing is ever safe. "*

Megan Glass
www.glasshousepuppies.com

Photo Courtesy of Maggie Box
www.angelviewdoodles.com

messes that can cause unnecessary stress. Whether it means choosing an empty room, buying a playpen, or rigging baby gates on every doorway, it's good to give your dog clear boundaries.

This space should contain fresh water, plenty of toys, and a crate for sleeping. While housetraining, puppies do well to sleep in a crate so they learn that they are supposed to sleep and stay quiet during the night. It can also help cut down on pet messes. Older Bernedoodles can enjoy crate time as well because it provides a safe, cozy spot to hide out in when they're feeling stressed.

Once your Bernedoodle matures, you can open up more of the house to it as you see fit. If there are rooms in the house where you would rather not let your dog go, like bedrooms, the baby gates can be moved to keep these places off-limits. Eventually, your Bernedoodle will learn where it is allowed to go and what areas it should avoid.

Because adult Bernedoodles need a lot of space to move around, a fenced-in backyard is necessary. Remember, your Bernedoodle will grow up to be a giant dog, so a short fence just won't cut it. It's best to surround your outdoor space with a six foot fence without any gaps that a dog can squeeze through. Your Bernedoodle may seem relaxed and easy going, but don't underestimate its ability to leap over a short fence or squeeze through a gap if something exciting is happening on the other side. Young dogs are notorious for running off to explore the world around them, and you don't want to run the risk of losing your pet.

If you plan on keeping your Bernedoodle outside for a large amount of time during the day, make sure that it is comfortable. Especially in warm weather,

Bernedoodles can become overheated. Make sure that there is ample shade and cool water for them. Also, you may want to choose a designated toilet area in your yard to make clean-up easier. Choose a spot out of the way of foot traffic, and bring your pup to that spot when it's time to do its business.

Especially at the beginning, it's good to create boundaries for your Bernedoodle. This allows it to learn how to respect your space and possessions. As time goes on, it'll begin to understand the rules and will be less likely to explore forbidden areas.

By the time you're ready to bring your new Bernedoodle home, you'll have everything ready to make sure your dog and your household are safe. Adding a new dog to the family can feel like a big transition, but there are resources out there that can help. Breeders, animal shelter employees, and veterinarians are all good sources to go to if you have any questions about making your home safe and comfortable for your new Bernedoodle.

Photo Courtesy of Alicia Marshall
"Highfalutin Furry Babies Bernedoodles"

CHAPTER 4

BRINGING HOME YOUR BERNEDOODLE

Once your house is prepared for the arrival of your new Bernedoodle, you're ready to bring your dog home. The transition to a new place can be stressful to a dog that may not know anything outside of its breeder's home. Especially if your household doesn't already have another dog, there are a lot of supplies to pur-

Photo Courtesy of Maggie Box
www.angelviewdoodles.com

chase and plans to put into place. This chapter is your guide for the first few days as a new Bernedoodle owner.

The First Day

Not all dogs enjoy car rides and you don't want your new pup's first experience with you to be a scary one. The journey home is a big transition. Your dog will be separated from people and other dogs that it knows. During the ride home, new dogs need a little extra comfort as they make their journey to their new house.

A good car ride experience can save you and your pet stress in the long run. A negative experience can possibly condition your dog to associate cars with fear. If cars become scary, it will be difficult to convince it to hop in the next time you want to go to the veterinarian or training class.

If possible, find someone to accompany you to pick up the Bernedoodle. If you're driving, it makes it harder to pay attention to the dog. Another passenger can help keep your Bernedoodle calm and comfortable. Petting the dog or speaking to it in a gentle voice can reassure it that everything will be okay.

Perhaps the safest way to transport a dog is in a crate. If not properly restrained, your dog could become seriously injured in the event of a car accident. Even a bump in the road could send a dog flying through the car. For everyone's safety, decide on a method of restraint before picking your dog up.

Crates are great because they provide a small space that can make a puppy feel at ease. The crates themselves can be securely fastened to the seat, so they can't budge. As an added bonus, if your dog has an accident or gets sick, it's much easier to clean up a plastic crate than the seat fabric.

The least-advised transport method is to let your dog move freely around the car. Even a well-trained dog can be unpredictable in a stressful situation. Not only is the dog at risk for being injured, but it's dangerous for the driver to deal with distractions. Your puppy might want to cuddle and climb around you as you drive, but it's extremely dangerous for everyone in the car.

Once you get home, it's time to let your dog check out its new home. Since its boundaries have already been decided, it probably won't have far to go. Let it check out where it will be sleeping and take it outside to see where it will be using the bathroom.

Introduce your dog to all of your family members. A new dog can be exciting, but try to keep everyone calm and relaxed. Let your dog sniff people out and give it a couple small treats. Give your dog sufficient exercise through lots of play time. If you have a puppy, chances are it will be exhausted from all of the excitement and will need a quick nap.

As much as you want to take your new dog everywhere with you, short breaks away from your dog are good. Most owners will eventually have to leave their dog home alone for at least a few hours each day, so you'll want to prepare your dog for that separation. It doesn't have to be more than a few minutes at first, but giving your dog a little alone time won't hurt it.

The first few nights with a new puppy can be tough. Your puppy is probably used to being surrounded by its siblings and mother. Suddenly, your dog is all alone in an unfamiliar place. It's bound to be tough on the little guy. It's hard to hear your dog so upset, but your family members have to sleep, too. What do you do?

If you're planning on crate training, your puppy should be put to bed every night in its crate. However, you may want to consider the best place for that crate at the beginning. New dog owners may be tempted to put their dog out of earshot, but that can make them even more uneasy. Some experts suggest putting the crate inside your bedroom or even just outside the door. This way, your dog knows that you're near and that it hasn't been completely abandoned.

Another reason for keeping the puppy near is so you know when it needs to be let outside. Puppies have tiny bladders, so there's a good chance it'll want to be let out during the night. Crying is its natural warning that something is wrong, so it will vocalize its needs to you. The crying may go on for a long time initially, but once it tires itself out, you'll be able to hear when it has settled down.

Your puppy's bedtime routine has an effect on how it sleeps through the night. Before putting your dog in its crate, take it on one last walk around the yard. Not only will it take this time to use the bathroom, it will also tire itself out by running around. It will probably still cry a little at first, but eventually it'll calm down enough to fall asleep.

The first few weeks may be tough on both puppy and owner, but once the puppy gets settled into a routine and becomes comfortable with being alone, it'll soon be sleeping through the night. Resist the urge to either store it in the basement to escape its cries or to cuddle it in bed with you. This stage will eventually pass and your Bernedoodle will be on its way to becoming fully housetrained.

Going to the Vet

If you signed a health guarantee with a breeder, going to the vet within the first few days of purchase is necessary to keep up your end of the agreement. Even if you got your Bernedoodle at a shelter, it's not a bad idea to have it checked out soon after it comes home. Dogs from shelters occasionally pick up illnesses from the other dogs they share a space with.

It's a good idea to choose a new vet before you bring your dog home, so you'll be prepared for any sudden illness or injury. You want someone who is trustworthy,

Photo Courtesy of Ariel Leon

is knowledgeable about your dog, and gets along well with both you and your Bernedoodle.

If you live in a city with lots of choices of veterinarians, it can be tough to pick one. In this case, it is good to talk to other pet owners and see where they take their pets. Your friends and coworkers can also give you some inside information about vets, facilities, and prices. Another safe bet is to see which vet your breeder goes to. If you got your Bernedoodle from a shelter, ask about the vet that they use.

Once you've narrowed down your search, check out a few clinics and see if you can get any more information from their websites. Lots of websites contain information about the employees and facilities. Look for veterinarians that specialize in dogs and understand the needs of your Bernedoodle. There, you can also see what their hours are. Check to see if their business hours work with your daily schedule. You will also need to know what their protocol is in case of an emergency.

Next, make a few visits to your top choices. Your clinic should let you have a brief tour of their facilities. First, you'll want to make sure the clinic is clean. Make sure it is free of odors and bodily fluids, for your dog's safety as well as your own. If pos-

Photo Courtesy of Ariel Leon

sible, try to observe how the employees interact with the animals. You want employees who are kind, attentive, and knowledgeable.

Next, see what kinds of tests and procedures the facilities allow. They should have several exam rooms, a laboratory for running tests, an x-ray room, and surgery rooms. If they have all of these rooms, there's a good chance that they'll provide all of the services you may need for your Bernedoodle. Smaller offices often refer their clients to other labs or hospitals for procedures that their facilities cannot handle. You must decide if this makes a difference to you. Sometimes, having to send samples to other labs can delay a diagnosis.

Try to meet with a vet that specializes in dog medicine. You can ask a few questions to gauge his or her knowledge of the breed. Mostly, this meeting is to see if you get along, since you'll be visiting a few times a year. Even if your dog doesn't necessarily require a checkup or vaccinations right away, it's not a bad idea to introduce your dog to the vet. Make it a positive experience with lots of treats and praise and it might even enjoy its regular visit to the vet.

Finding a new vet is an important part of preparing your home for a Bernedoodle. When illness or injury occur unexpectedly, you'll want someone you can trust to take care of your dog. Veterinarians are an invaluable resource when you have questions about caring for your new dog.

Pet Supplies

Another necessary part of being prepared for a new dog is having all of the right supplies. Going to a pet store can be overwhelming because there are so many different products on the market. After a while, buying new things for your Bernedoodle can add up. There are some supplies that are absolutely necessary for your dog's wellbeing, and other products that are nice extras. Here are some things to pick up at the pet store before your Bernedoodle comes home.

First, you'll need somewhere for your dog to sleep. Crates are perfect for this because they also provide a cozy relaxation space for your dog and they are perfect for transporting your Bernedoodle in the car. Crates are most commonly made out of wood, wire, or plastic. Wire crates are good for letting your dog see its surroundings and provide good air flow, but they may need to be covered at night for optimum sleeping. Plastic crates are easy to clean, but it's good to find one that your Bernedoodle can't sink its teeth into.

Your dog's crate should be large enough that it can stand up and turn around inside of it. However, it shouldn't be too large, or else puppies won't have any problem using it for a bathroom. Dogs generally don't like to potty where they sleep, so a properly sized crate will help keep them from making messes. Because there is a large size range between the Bernedoodle puppy and adult, you may find it necessary to own more than one crate as it grows.

Especially if you're bringing home a puppy, it's good to have a few baby gates or a play pen on hand. If you give your new dog the run of the house, don't be surprised when you find messes in unexpected places. Giving your dog its own space makes it easier to keep an eye on it until you know that its destructive behaviors are under control. Plus, having a special area keeps it safe by separating it from other dangers in your home.

Next, your Bernedoodle needs two bowls for food and water. There are so many different types of bowls on the market that it can be hard to pick one. A good, sturdy stainless steel bowl is hard to beat because it's durable and easy to clean. Make sure the water bowl is kept full of clean, fresh water at all times, and the food bowl is only full during meal times.

In order to keep your Bernedoodle safe, you need a good collar and leash. Most dogs do well with a thick, flat collar that fastens with a buckle. These can easily be adjusted as your dog grows, A good fitting collar should be snug enough that your dog can't slip out, but loose enough that it doesn't cause discomfort. If you can slide two fingers under the collar, it's a good fit. Alternatively, some dogs, especially shelter dogs, have throat problems that make collars painful. A harness is a good choice if collars aren't an option for your dog. Whichever you choose, make sure to keep identification tags and license tags on at all times. When choosing a leash, pick something strong like leather or nylon. Choose a four foot or six foot leash, because shorter leashes make training easier than long retractable ones.

Your new dog will also need a few toys to keep it happy and entertained. Bernedoodles are big dogs that need sturdy toys that can't easily be destroyed. When searching for new toys, make sure there aren't any parts that can easily break off and choke your dog. Also, make sure nothing will splinter and puncture any of your dog's internal organs if swallowed. Tough, rubber toys and bones designed specifically for your dog's oral health are safe bets. If you have any concerns, ask a breeder or vet what they recommend.

You'll also want to pick up a few grooming supplies to have on hand. Brushes, nail trimmers, and a toothbrush and toothpaste are necessary for keeping your dog looking good and feeling healthy. Depending on whether you're planning on bathing your dog at home or visiting a groomer, you may also want to have a gentle shampoo.

Of course, you'll also need to have some food on hand. Before you purchase a food, it's important to find out what your Bernedoodle was eating at its last home. A sudden switch in foods can cause stomach upset, or just make it turn up its little nose. If you're planning on switching dog foods, slowly transition by mixing the familiar food with the new food. Treats are also good to have for welcoming your new dog into your home and for training rewards.

The Cost Breakdown

Owning a dog is a huge commitment. As an owner, you must be able to cover the cost of keeping your dog healthy and happy for its entire life. While the initial cost of bringing a new dog home can be shocking, keep in mind that there will also be some expenses that continue for the rest of your dog's life. Of course, the cost of your individual Bernedoodle may vary depending on where you live, but here are some estimates to consider before deciding if you can afford a Bernedoodle.

First, consider how much it will cost to get your Bernedoodle in the first place. If you're buying a puppy from a breeder, expect to pay somewhere between $1,000 to over $3,000. If you're going to adopt, fees will be around the $200-$400 range.

When you first bring your dog home, there will be a lot of one-time expenses. Toys, grooming products, a crate, gates, and other things will add up quickly. Expect to pay around $200 for necessary items. Training is another one-time expense if you choose to hire a professional or attend a class. These cost anywhere from $100-$500 for basic obedience training.

Yearly vet bills may cost somewhere between $200-$400 depending on what services are performed. A Bernedoodle from a good breeder should run into few health problems, but regular checkups and vaccinations are still necessary for good health.

Bernedoodles are big dogs, so they need to eat more food than most breeds. The cost of dog food is a huge variable because there are so many to choose from. The average dog eats about $300 worth of food in a year. Depending on how big your Bernedoodle gets and how expensive your preferred food is, it could easily be more than that.

Depending on all of the economic choices you make for your dog, the cost adds up quickly. If you get your Bernedoodle when it's a puppy, a lifetime of care could run you somewhere in the range of $10,000 on the cheap end, and up to $40,000.

This may seem excessive, but don't fret—when you consider how much it cost to care for a human child, it's quite doable in comparison. Besides, once you have your Bernedoodle in your arms, you'll find that you'll pay any amount to make sure they are as happy as can be!

There is a lot of preparation involved when it's time to bring your new friend home, but its first experiences of its new home really makes a big impact on its growth and development. Having everything ready for your dog will make both you and your dog happier. Once your pup is settled in, that's when the fun really starts.

Photo Courtesy of Maggie Box
www.angelviewdoodles.com

CHAPTER 5

HOW TO BE A PUPPY PARENT

Photo Courtesy of Maggie Box
www.angelviewdoodles.com

Owning a Bernedoodle is a big commitment. It involves an extra commitment of funds, time, and work to make your dog a productive member of your household. If you let it, your Bernedoodle will waltz into your home and set its own rules. However, your dog's ideas about acceptable behavior may differ from yours. If you don't take the time to observe your dog's natural behaviors and correct the bad habits, don't be surprised when it rips your couch the shreds while you are away at work.

But, before you demand certain behaviors from your dog, you must have a clear idea of what your behavioral expectations are. For example, you shouldn't teach your Bernedoodle that the sofa is off limits, only to call it up to cuddle with you while you watch television. This will lead to confusion for your dog and frustration for you when your dog doesn't do what you want.

If you share your home with other humans, make sure to discuss rules that you'd like your dog to follow. That way, someone else isn't allowing your dog on the bed when you told your dog no. It is far easier to train your dog using teamwork, as opposed to having family members sabotage your hard work.

Also, remember that dogs don't remember things in the same way that humans do. If you were teaching a child right from wrong, you could explain to them why coloring on the wall is not good, even hours after the fact. With a dog, you can lead them back to the hole they dug earlier in the day, and they're more inclined to think, "Hey, that's a nice hole", instead of feeling sorry for destroying your yard. Dogs can only be corrected in the moment they make the mistake, so it's important to keep a close watch on your dog, especially early on.

It can be hard to tell your dog not to do something, especially when it looks up at your with its big, Bernedoodle puppy eyes. Stay strong—it's easier to stop bad behaviors before they become bad habits. You may feel guilty for telling your pup no, but it will make for a much happier household if you do. Be firm, but kind. Your puppy is still developing, so be prepared for mistakes. Staying calm and patient will get you through the new puppy stage. While you may come up with many different rules for your dog, here are some common behavioral issues and tips for working though them.

Chewing

Chewing is a common problem amongst new puppy owners. There are several reasons why your Bernedoodle might chew on your belongings. Dogs are curious creatures and one way they take in the world is through taste. If your new dog wants to learn what something is, it will sniff and taste it. Dogs use their sense of taste and touch through their mouths.

If your Bernedoodle is a puppy, there's a good chance that its teeth are causing it some discomfort. Just like with human babies, dog babies need a way to push their new teeth through their gums. Plus, chewing can provide relief to sore mouths.

The other reasons your dog might chew are mostly behavioral. If your dog is feeling neglected, bored, or anxious, it may chew to relieve anxiety or to gain attention. For these issues, try to find the root of your dog's unhappiness. A little extra play time, more obedience training, or just some extra cuddles can help resolve the problems. Then, you can work on teaching your dog that chewing is not an appropriate way to express its unhappiness. If your dog is showing signs of anxiety, talk to your vet about ways to ease its symptoms.

Regardless of whether your dog has toys or not, it is inclined to sink its teeth into something. If you'd rather it not be your furni-

Photo Courtesy of Charlene Waggert

ture, supply your dog with an array of fun toys to keep it entertained. Sturdy rubber toys and bones designed for chewing are good options. Avoid any toys that can easily be ripped to shreds and ingested.

Make sure your dog can tell the difference between its toys and your possessions. If you notice that your puppy likes to nibble on your shoes, don't give it an old shoe as a compromise. Chances are, it won't be able to tell the difference, and will learn that all shoes make good chew toys.

In the early days, follow your dog closely to catch it in the act of misbehaving. When you witness undesirable behavior, make a noise that catches its attention. A firm "hey" can clue it in to the fact that you're not happy with what it's doing. Once it stops, give it a toy to chew on. If it drops your belongings and takes the toy, reward it with praise.

For more persistent pets that love to gnaw on furniture, there are products on the market that work as taste deterrents. These sprays are safe for dogs to lick but taste bad, so they'll learn not to chew. When trying out a taste deterrent, purchase from a pet store or ask a vet first. Avoid "natural" deterrents made from household items that you read about on the Internet—they aren't always safe for pets.

When teaching a dog not to chew on your belongings, never punish your dog after the fact. It won't remember what it did, which may confuse it as to why you're yelling. If your dog snatches your television remote, don't run after it. This will turn into a fun game of chase for your dog, and frustration for you.

Finally, expect your Bernedoodle to chew on something it's not supposed to chew on once or twice. When it happens, be patient and never physically punish your dog. It's frustrating to see your favorite throw pillows get ruined, but it's all part of being a puppy parent. Luckily, if you puppy-proof your home well enough, there won't be much for your dog to sink its teeth into!

Digging

It always seems as though the moment you finish planting flowers, your dog comes racing through the yard to dig up all of your hard work. There are different reasons why your Bernedoodle might enjoy digging up the yard. Bernedoodles are active dogs, so if they're left alone in a yard with no other entertainment, they may choose digging as a way to spend their excess energy. If boredom and excess energy cause a dog to dig, this can be remedied by making sure it has plenty of toys, or people, in the yard to play with. A long walk can also help them with extra energy.

Remember, smart dogs like Bernedoodles get bored more easily than other breeds. When an intelligent working dog gets bored, it makes up its own games and jobs. Digging is a common behavior seen in bored pups. Extra training helps keep its active mind focused.

Another reason dogs dig is because they're trying to reach the cool earth for some relief from the heat. Bernedoodles have a lot of heavy fur, so they overheat easily. If your Bernedoodle tends to dig holes on hot days, make sure it has a cool place to hang out. Bernedoodles need sufficient shade and plenty of cool water when it's warm. Pay close attention to its behavior when the weather is hot. If your Bernedoodle appears especially lethargic, let it spend some time inside with the air conditioning on.

Dogs with high prey drives may also dig up a yard, especially if there are smaller critters burrowing underground. They may think they're doing a good job, when in reality, they are making a mess. If you discover vermin in your yard, be careful with how you choose to eliminate them, because traps and poisons are often extremely dangerous for dogs.

Some dogs just love to dig. If you try to pinpoint the cause of your dog's digging and can't find a solution, you may need to create an acceptable place for your Bernedoodle to perform its favorite task. When you catch your dog digging, get its attention. Then, direct your dog to a sandbox or designated digging zone and praise it when it digs in the correct spot. Supervise your dog the first few times, until it has a good grasp of where it's allowed to dig, and where is off-limits.

Growling and Barking

It can get annoying if your Bernedoodle barks at every passerby, or just likes the sounds of its own voice. It's normal for all dogs to bark every now and again. Bernedoodles are protective dogs, so they might try to warn you if they believe an intruder is near. However, excessive barking isn't necessary and can cause stress within a home. To stop your dog's excessive barking, learn the cause of its barking and work out a solution for the problem.

Most often, a dog barks because it learns that making noise gets it attention. If it barks and someone speaks to it or starts petting it to get it to stop, then it thinks that using its voice is a good way to be noticed. Even your yelling can be seen as attention. If your dog barks for the attention, try ignoring it until it calms down on its own. Reward it when it's finally silent.

Photo Courtesy of Alicia Marshall
"Highfalutin Furry Babies Bernedoodles"

Another common behavior is barking at an outside stimulus. Usually, this comes in the form of a friendly mail carrier walking past the window, or someone ringing the doorbell. If the outside world sends your dog into hysterics, one thing you can do is remove or desensitize it to the stimulus.

This may take some extra work. Use a family member or friend to practice with you by standing within sight of your dog. If your Bernedoodle stays calm and quiet, reward it with treats. If your dog barks, ignore it and do not give out treats. With practice, your dog will learn that they are not supposed to bark at people approaching the house.

Another tactic is to give a special command when someone is at the door. If it is instructed to go to its crate or lie down on its bed when someone approaches the house, it will be too distracted by its job to bark.

Growling is another story. While dogs often bark just to elicit a response from their people, growling serves a very specific purpose. When a dog growls, it's communicating that it's very upset, to the point of snapping. When you hear a Bernedoodle's warning growl, figure out the source of the stress. Once you know what makes your dog growl, find ways to avoid its stressors or work on cautiously changing its behavior through socialization.

Separation Anxiety

66 *For me it is important that folks understand that these dogs are not a 'backyard' dog. They crave and need human interaction. If you cannot provide that then the Bernedoodle is not your breed."*

Diane Caldemeyer-Reid
www.vonfarawayfarms.com

Separation anxiety occurs when your Bernedoodle becomes traumatized from being left alone. Serious anxiety in dogs can wreak havoc on their mental and physical health over time. If you notice your puppy is misbehaving, try to figure out if its apparent naughtiness is just a result of anxiety.

Some symptoms of separation anxiety include: destructive behaviors, urinating and defecating indoors, pacing, attempts to escape, crying or excessive barking, and unexplained panting. If your dog only has these problems while you're away or about to leave, then it likely suffers from separation anxiety.

Photo Courtesy of Carol Heller
www.highmesadoodles.com

This is found most commonly in puppies because they aren't used to spending time alone. Going from a breeder's house with its siblings and mother to a stranger's house can be traumatizing. Adjusting your new puppy to your absence is an important first step of dog ownership.

The key is to start slow and build up your time away from your dog incrementally. Start by going into another room for a few minutes while your puppy plays by itself. Then, you can build up to longer periods of time until your pup feels more comfortable. After that, the next step is to leave the home. Start by taking an hour or two away to run errands, until you're able to leave the home for extended periods of time without causing panic.

Avoid making a big production of your comings and goings. If you give your dog a big hug and speak to it in a high-pitched voice every time you walk out the door, it will see your departure as a big deal. Similarly, if you demand an enthusiastic greeting when you return, the dog will associate it with your departure. Leave and return calmly and casually, and suddenly, and your leaving will hardly faze it.

To make things easier on your pooch, make sure it has plenty of entertainment in your absence. Toys and treats are great for distracting your dog from its anxiety. If your pup is crate trained, its crate can be a comforting place for it to go while it's alone. If all else fails, try taking your Bernedoodle puppy on a nice, long walk before leaving it alone. It might be too pooped to worry about your absence.

Sometimes, a dog's anxiety is too severe for just treats and toys. If you've been working with your dog and its separation anxiety for a long time and it isn't showing any improvement, talk to your vet. He or she may be able to give you advice for helping ease your dog's symptoms, and, if absolutely necessary, may also give your dog a prescription anti-anxiety medicine.

Running Away

Many new dog owners will find that their curious pup likes to escape from their home and go on an adventure through the neighborhood. Unfortunately, the free world is filled with dangers that your Bernedoodle needs protection from. Also, if your new dog isn't familiar with the area, it may get lost all too easily. The urge to run off is strongest in dogs that haven't been neutered, so keep a close watch on your little male until you can have him neutered.

Most of the time, dogs run away because they have a lot of energy and they want a fun, exciting activity to keep them entertained. If an ignored dog feels like it can find attention elsewhere, it is more inclined to bolt the first time it gets the chance. If your dog is a ball of energy, it may discover that it can stretch its legs better on a wide open street than it can in a small yard.

If your dog is a runner, address the cause. Does it have sufficient exercise and attention? If your gate has gaps or is too short, something exciting, like a squirrel, may prompt it to chase. Especially with a new dog, a change of scene may make it want to check out its environment. A dog that previously lived on a farm or that lived in another home may just want to go back to what it knows as home. Until it settles down, make sure it doesn't get the chance to run.

In the meantime, work on commands for exiting and entering the house. Have your dog sit before opening the gate, and work on a command to call it back in. That way, when it's gearing up to run, it knows that it has to complete a task before it can leave.

Bedtime

Just as you would do with young children, you need to give your young pup a set bedtime routine. Good bedtime habits ensure that your dog sleeps well, which in turn ensures good sleep for the owner.

At first, bedtime can be tricky for a new puppy. It isn't used to being alone, which can trigger crying. It's hard to hear your new puppy cry all night, but it has to be able to fall asleep on its own, assuming that it won't be permanently sleeping on your bed.

Make sure your pup has a cozy, comfortable place to sleep. Crates are great places for dogs to sleep because a covered crate can help eliminate any distractions that can keep your dog up at night. Give it a soft bed or blanket to sleep on, and make sure your home isn't too cold.

Next, create a bedtime routine. Avoid feeding your puppy too late in the day because it needs plenty of time to digest its food. Before bedtime, give your Bernedoodle ample time to use the bathroom. One of the biggest reasons puppies cry at night is because they need to relieve themselves. Once it is finished, bring it inside and instruct it to lie down on its bed. At this time, it's important to go to bed as well, so it doesn't see you and decide it wants to play. The first thing in the morning, take it outside to use the bathroom again. Especially for puppies, eight hours is a very long time to hold it.

If you still have problems getting your Bernedoodle to settle down at night, make sure it is getting enough exercise during the day. A tired dog is more likely to sleep during the night because it needs its rest to regain strength. Shoot for a long walk in the early evening, that way its energy has been spent, yet it isn't wound up too close to bedtime.

The puppy stage is a difficult time for both owner and pup. It's a time of transition, so extra patience is needed. Make sure you have clear rules and expectations for your Bernedoodle so it doesn't get confused about what you want. After a month or two of hard work, your Bernedoodle will be comfortable in your home.

Photo Courtesy of Maggie Box
www.angelviewdoodles.com

CHAPTER 6

HOUSETRAINING

Photo Courtesy of Carol Heller
www.highmesadoodles.com

" *You will want to use a command such as "Go potty" every time you take them out and when they go potty and you will want to praise them when they go with something like "Good dog". Consistency is key; if you are not consistent you cannot blame the dog if they do not understand what you are trying to get them to do."*

Carol Heller
www.highmesadoodles.com

Housetraining is an essential part of dog ownership if you are planning on allowing your Bernedoodle to spend any length of time in the house. This breed needs this option because they get lonely easily.

Just like any other puppy behavior, your new Bernedoodle might not understand that it isn't allowed to use the bathroom where it pleases. If your Bernedoodle came from a knowledgeable breeder, the breeder may have already started housetraining the puppies. However, the concept will still be very new, so more work is required.

One reason that housetraining is so difficult to start is that your tiny pup doesn't have the bladder capacity yet to hold it for any great length of time. Typically, puppies can hold their bladders one hour for every month old they are. For example, if you have a two-month-old Bernedoodle, it probably needs to go out to do its business every two hours.

Housetraining Options

Depending on your home and schedule, there are different options for house-training that won't result in ruined carpet. Using a designated spot outside is per-haps the most ideal method because your dog is less likely to be confused by your expectations for it. It can easily tell the difference between the backyard and the liv-ing room, so once it's let outside, it knows it's allowed to use the bathroom. Owners may also find they prefer to only allow their dog to potty outside because it keeps the pet messes out of the home altogether.

However, if certain circumstances make this impossible for you and your pup, there are other options. You may decide to teach your puppy to do its business on a designated indoor spot while you're away, and to use the yard when you're home. For inside training, there are a few different choices. Using newspaper is a fairly common (and cheap) method, but it can result in messes if the layer of paper isn't thick enough to absorb the urine.

Potty pads are another popular product. Think of them as large, absorbent dia-pers that adhere to your floor. Many contain a scent that is supposed to let your dog

Photo Courtesy of Alicia Marshall
"Highfalutin Furry Babies Bernedoodles"

know that they are meant to be used as a toilet. They are disposable, so clean up is easy. Because they are not reusable, prolonged use can be expensive and not great for the environment. However, as a backup method for dogs that are inside all day while the family is away, they can help contain accidents.

Dog owners looking for a more permanent indoor toilet may choose a dog litter box or a box that can be covered in turf or sod to mimic an outdoor toilet. These methods are best suited for small dogs and puppies, so your Bernedoodle may not be able to use them for too long before it reaches its adult size.

If you decide to go with an indoor potty, placement is important. Find a space in your home where messes won't interfere with your life. Also, don't place a pad in an inconvenient place, just because your dog fancies that place for a toilet. For example, your puppy may like to do its business in the middle of your kitchen floor, but it's not a sanitary place to have those messes. Put a pad as far away from living spaces as possible, in a place like the bathroom, and teach your dog to go there.

However, if you don't want your dog to become comfortable using your home as a toilet, you may want to avoid training it to use alternative methods altogether. This is entirely possible if you are capable of taking your dog outside every few hours during its puppy stage. As it grows up, letting it out during a lunch break or with a dog walker may be sufficient for its needs.

The First Few Months

Housetraining is a lot of work. Expect your puppy to need constant practice in appropriate elimination methods for several months. Because Bernedoodles mature a little slower than most breeds, this time can vary.

A good way to prevent accidents in the home is to set a routine for your pup. When you wake up in the morning (which will probably be early with a new dog) take your puppy to its designated bathroom spot outside. Once it has used the bathroom, then it's breakfast time. Because dogs should have set feeding times anyway, its next bowel movement will be a little more predictable. Let your dog out within thirty minutes of finishing its meal.

From there, determine how long your dog is capable of holding it. If you notice that your dog has accidents at a certain time interval after being let out last, schedule a bathroom break a little earlier. If you watch your puppy closely, you can start to see patterns in its behavior and can anticipate its needs a little better. For example, if your puppy is having accidents an hour after its last bathroom break, try letting it out every forty-five minutes and work on increasing the time between.

It's also a good idea to take your puppy outside after a nap and right before bedtime. After a while, the routine will start to stick and your puppy will understand what it is supposed to do while outside.

It can be difficult to predict when your puppy is about to use the bathroom. Some dogs give little to no warning before they make a mess on your floor. Others may whine, walk around in small circles, or scratch at the ground. If you notice any of these warning signs, bring your puppy to the yard as quickly as possible so it can learn where it is supposed to go.

Make sure you have some consistency with where you take your dog once you get outside. If you take your dog to the same outdoor spot every time, eventually, the scent it leaves behind will prompt it to do its business. This is an added bonus for the owner because it makes clean up easier and reduces the risk of soiling a pair of shoes.

Positive Reinforcement while Housetraining

Because housetraining is one of the first things new owners work on with their dogs, it's important to get into the habit of using positive reinforcement. Dogs respond well to positive feedback in the form of treats and affection. Negative feedback, like fear, pain, or intimidation, will only lead to resentment and fear from your dog. In fact, negative reinforcement will likely result in unwanted behaviors.

When your dog decides it's time to go to the bathroom, lead it to its designated toilet area. When it uses the bathroom successfully, give it a treat. This lets it know that it performed its job correctly. Give your Bernedoodle plenty of cuddles and let it know that it did well. After enough of these positive experiences, it will understand what you want it to do.

Photo Courtesy of Marva Smith

If you take your dog out and it doesn't use the bathroom, give it a little time. Perhaps it needs to sniff around for a little while longer. Try to remove any distractions so it knows that it's outside for business, not play. Keep toys and other people out of reach at this time. If your Bernedoodle tries to play with you while outside, act uninterested. Eventually, it will figure out that you aren't there to play. Stay still and quiet, and just observe so you're ready with treats when your dog is finished.

In the Event of an Accident

Photo Courtesy of Charlene Waggert

Accidents happen—and a puppy is bound to have quite a few. This is completely normal and to be expected. Because negative reinforcement doesn't work well with dogs, they should never be punished for an accident, especially after the fact. Dogs cannot connect past mistakes to the present. Even rubbing their nose in their mess won't cause them to remember that what they did was wrong. Yelling and swatting at your dog will cause it to see the act of eliminating waste as wrong. Instead of waiting to go outside, a scared dog is more likely to hide it from you, causing even bigger issues.

Unfortunately, if you don't catch your dog in the act, you've lost out on a learning moment. While it may seem discouraging when you've been working with your dog for months, stay patient. Your dog will need to go in another hour or two, giving you another chance to try to make it outside.

If you do catch it, try to startle but not scare the dog by giving a single clap or a "hey!" This isn't meant to be mean or frighten it, but should work as an alarm of sorts. If the noise distracts it enough that it stops, quickly bring your dog outside to its bathroom spot. If it completes the task outside, reward it. If it doesn't, try again later. Bernedoodles are eager to please their owners, so positive reinforcement works especially well, and negative reinforcement is especially damaging for your dog.

If your dog has reached a mature age and is still having accidents despite all of the work you've put in, consider other factors that may be causing the accidents. Male dogs that have not been neutered yet may use urine as a way to mark their territory. Some dogs will void their bladders if they get too excited or anxious. Work with your dog's needs to resolve these behaviors and see if they become more successful with housetraining.

Crate Training

One of the benefits of crate training your dog is that it helps with the housetraining process. As a dog matures, it's less likely to use the bathroom in its living space. A crate provides an enclosed area that your dog may be more inclined to keep clean.

This is beneficial for dog owners who struggle with their dog having accidents at night and while they're not around. If the dog hangs out in the crate when it cannot be closely supervised, it may avoid having accidents that way.

❝ *Crate training is very important as dogs are den animals and need a place of safety. This will also help with potty training as it helps them to hold their potty for a long period of time. You will want to take your new puppy out every two hours to go potty during the day."*

Carol Heller
www.highmesadoodles.com

Photo Courtesy of Alex Byrnes

If the crate is too big, there is ample room for a puppy to poop on one side and sleep on the other. A proper-fitting crate eliminates that excess room. Once you let the dog out of the crate, immediately take it outside to eliminate waste.

Avoid keeping potty pads or newspaper in the crate if your dog associates them with using the bathroom. If accidents occur, wash whatever bedding is in there and try again. Specially made enzymatic cleansers are good for removing the smells that make animals use the bathroom in certain areas.

Doggy Doors

There are both benefits and disadvantages to installing a doggy door in your home. On the plus side, having a little door for your Bernedoodle to go outside when nature calls is great for owners who can't be home during the day. If your dog can use the bathroom outside on its own time, it probably won't have accidents in the home.

But in order for your dog to be able to use a doggy door, it must be house-trained well enough to know the purpose of going outside. A pup that doesn't know that it's supposed to use the bathroom outside won't suddenly become house-trained, just because it has unlimited access to the outside. A young dog may also be too scared of the door to actually use it. However, once your pup is trained, a doggy door can give it a little more independence.

Another drawback to using doggy doors is that the owner has less control over what comes in and goes out of the house. A sneaky dog can take its favorite toys or its owner's possessions with it, without anyone noticing. Also, if your dog can get inside, so can other small creatures, not to mention any fresh kills your dog may have made while outside.

Housetraining Adult Dogs

Most often, housebreaking is a puppy issue. However, if you adopt an adult Bernedoodle, it might not be housetrained already. If the Bernedoodle spent most of its time outside in its former home, it may have never learned how to use the bathroom in specific places.

The guidelines for housetraining adult dogs are similar to those for training puppies. They need lots of positive reinforcement when they use the bathroom in the correct spot and they require plenty of practice.

After your dog completes its task, a walk is a good reward. It makes it happy, plus it will be more likely to take care of business immediately so it can have fun afterwards.

The best thing about housetraining an older dog is that it doesn't need to use the bathroom as often as a puppy. Instead of taking your dog out every hour, it can go out once in the morning, once at bedtime, and a handful of times throughout the day. Once it gets the hang of it, it will only need to be let out four or five times a day.

Housetraining is difficult at first, but once your Bernedoodle gets the hang of it, your life will become much easier. Bernedoodles are intelligent, but mature a little slower than most dogs, so remember to be patient and keep training positive. They can be sensitive to negative reactions from their owner, so only reinforce behaviors with treats, cuddles, and play time, not anger.

Photo Courtesy of Megan Glass
www.glasshousepuppies.com

CHAPTER 7

SOCIALIZING YOUR BERNEDOODLE

Once your Bernedoodle is settled into your home, it's time to let it experience the world. Spending time on walks, at dog parks, and even trips to the vet are all enhanced by good social skills. Socialization means exposing your puppy to new experiences in order to make it feel more comfortable. The world can be a new and scary place for a pup, but having a good owner to show it the ropes can put its little mind at ease. Have your Bernedoodle get used to being around different types of people and animals from a young age, and you'll end up with a happy and well adjusted dog.

The Importance of Socialization

Good socialization can have a beneficial effect on your dog's physical health. When a dog gets scared or stressed by outside factors like other dogs or trips to the vet, it ignites a response to preserve its own life. When it senses danger, the flight or fight response kicks in to protect itself. As humans, we know that the friendly veterinarian isn't going to hurt it, but your Bernedoodle might not know that.

When those danger hormones kick in, they are preparing your dog to either fight for its life, or bolt. While these stress hormones can save your dog's life in the event of a real danger, it serves no purpose to its irrational fears. The hormones travel through the blood and pass through the kidneys while causing harm to internal organs. If this happens frequently, it can cause damage to your dog's immune system, making it more susceptible to disease and infection. Over time, stress that could easily be avoided can make your dog ill.

Proper socialization also keeps others safe around your dog. When a dog is stressed and scared, one natural reaction is to snap at people. Biting can protect it in case of an attack, but it not useful when someone's just trying to pet your dog.

In certain instances, like visiting the vet or a groomer, this fear can cause both the caregiver and your animal harm. If a veterinarian is trying to examine your dog, and it is unable to sit still out of fear, the vet cannot give you a good assessment, and a diagnosis might be missed. Similarly, your groomer may use sharp objects so if your dog can't hold still it may get a poke.

If your dog does not feel comfortable around anyone but you, it makes leaving it in the care of others very difficult. A kennel may send a nervous dog into hysterics, and if you hire a dog sitter, it may treat him or her like a dangerous intruder. It can be hard to leave a nervous dog in someone else's care, which means you might not be able to travel without your dog.

When a dog cannot interact with other people or dogs, it can be dangerous for everyone involved if the dog enters a situation it does not want to be in. Not only is it putting unnecessary stress on your dog's system, someone may be bitten when the dog finally snaps.

On the other hand, a well-socialized dog is a joy for everyone to be around. It's great knowing that other people can trust your dog and your dog can trust others. You won't have to worry about taking your dog out into public and it will be happy to see the world and everyone in it. A socialized dog will have a much better quality of life than an unsocialized dog.

Interacting with Other Dogs

If you don't already have another dog, you may wonder why it's necessary to show your dog how to behave around other dogs. Many dogs don't get a lot of interaction with others of their species. However, if you take your Bernedoodle outside

Photo Courtesy of Charlene Waggert

" *Like their parent breed, the Bernese Mountain Dog, Bernedoodles can be extremely sensitive, especially as young adults. "*

Megan Glass
www.glasshousepuppies.com

Photo Courtesy of Maggie Box

of your home, chances are you'll probably meet up with another dog at some point. If your dog has never interacted with another dog, it might not know how to react.

To understand the importance of socializing your dog with other dogs, it helps to understand how dogs interact with one another. If you go to a dog park, it's comforting to know when your dog is just playing and when you need to intervene. When you know what to look for when your dog is interacting with others, it gives the owner a little peace of mind to know that their precious pup is just doing what dogs do.

Though they don't vocalize like humans do, dogs communicate with others through their body gestures. Dogs are very sociable creatures—they like to live in packs. A dog that's used to being around other dogs will likely join in on the play.

Dog behaviors are often classified as being dominant or submissive. This isn't necessarily a positive or negative thing, and the roles can switch depending on which dogs are interacting. Some common shows of dominance include putting paws on another dog's back, humping, tail up, and general alertness. A submissive dog will stay low to the ground and might even roll over and expose its belly. Just because a dog is submissive around others doesn't necessarily mean that it is anxious or afraid.

There are some cues that may suggest a dog is anxious around others. Intense panting (not related to exercise), yawning, ears pinned back against the head, and a tucked tail all suggest that a dog is afraid. When a dog is tense, bares its teeth, and stares at the other dog, it may be gearing up for a fight. Alternatively, if the dog makes a bowing motion where the front of it is low and its bottom is in the air, it is inviting others to play with it.

Dogs communicate a lot by their sense of smell. If you've watched dogs greet one another, you know that they give each other a good sniff. While scientists don't know exactly what kind of information is being transferred, we know that dogs can smell the sex of another dog. In the wild, a male may need to be able to smell another male to know if he is in competition for mating. Even though many dogs in the park are neutered and not able to mate, their brains are still hardwired to sniff out the competition.

The best time to introduce your dog to other dogs is when it is still a puppy. It may be harder to socialize it when it gets older because it may already be apprehensive of other dogs. A puppy training class or a dog park are two great places to let your dog interact with a wide variety of dogs. If your dog is timid, you can try organizing play dates with friends' dogs. This is also easier on a nervous owner because you have more control over who gets to interact with your Bernedoodle.

In general, Bernedoodles tend to get along well with other dogs. They have the tendency to be shy, but once they have a little experience, they'll be playing with the other dogs in no time.

Socializing Your New Dog with Current Pets

Socializing your new Bernedoodle is especially important if it's going to be part of a larger family of pets! There's a little more at stake here because unlike play dates, there isn't the same option of leaving the party. If you've gotten to the point where you've decided to bring a new dog into the family, then you've probably determined that your other pets are friendly around dogs.

First, choose a neutral location for the meeting. Dogs can be territorial, so you don't want them to feel like they have anything they need to defend. Once they seem comfortable around each other, have them meet at home. Supervise them closely until you are certain that they can get along. It's best to keep them separated during this stage while you're not around to watch them. For example, utilize your puppy gates to give them the space they need.

Eventually, the dogs should get to the point within a few weeks where they can interact with each other without supervision. There should not be any signs of aggression from either dog. If you find that after a long time your dogs do not get along, you may wish to consult with a behavior specialist.

When introducing your new Bernedoodle to cats, the same general rules apply. Start very slow and leave plenty of space between the dog and cat. This may take a little more time, so be patient. The goal here is to get the Bernedoodle to the point where they aren't interested in the cat and won't bother it.

A more detailed look at adding a new dog to your pet family can be found in the next chapter.

Introducing Your Dog to Other People

❝ *The ideal home for a Bernedoodle is one where their family loves being with them as much as possible. If you do not spend time with your dog they can become skittish and shy away from people. Dogs do the best when they are well socialized."*

Carol Heller
www.highmesadoodles.com

When interacting with people, you want your Bernedoodle to be calm, yet happy. You don't want a fearful dog that barks or runs away from strangers. On the other hand, you don't want a dog that is overly excited and jumps on houseguests.

A good place to start this type of socialization is in your own home. People love meeting new puppies, so this is a chance to have friends over to introduce them to your Bernedoodle and vice versa. If your dog is skittish, keep it in a separate space until the people arrive. That way, it won't experience the anxiety of people ringing the doorbell and approaching the house.

Keep it slow and positive. Let your dog approach your guests. If someone reaches out for an uneasy dog, this may frighten it more. When it's feeling comfortable, it will approach people. Good behavior needs to be rewarded. If playtime and affection aren't enough, have your guests feed your Bernedoodle treats if it is calm.

Bernedoodles aren't typically aggressive around people, but sometimes poor breeding or bad past experiences can make your dog fearful of humans. If your particular Bernedoodle shows aggressive behaviors, have it meet people outside of the home. That way, it's less likely to feel territorial.

Never force your dog to socialize with someone if it is really unhappy. Instead, gradually let it get comfortable with the idea of being in the vicinity of other people first. Then, you may allow someone to hold the leash while walking together. After time, your Bernedoodle may feel comfortable enough to allow people to pet it.

It's fairly common for Bernedoodles to want to bark at people at the door. They are protective dogs and just want their people to know that someone is approaching their territory. While your dog might not mean any harm, it's not a desirable behavior for most homes. Have it get used to people at the door by staying calm when someone rings the doorbell. Speaking in a high-pitched, excited voice to your dog when someone arrives will only encourage this behavior. Instead, teach it to lie down on its bed when someone comes to the door. That way, it's too distracted to bark, and is in a safe place for being around new visitors.

63

Introducing Children to Your New Bernedoodle

" *The Bernese is one of the best companion dogs in the world. They are sweet, loving and loyal to a fault. After raising Bernese Mountain dogs for years and having owned them for over 25 years I can safely say that there is something special that grabs your heart and holds on forever."*

Diane Caldemeyer-Reid
www.vonfarawayfarms.com

This is a similar concept to introducing your dog to adults with a few extra considerations to make. Many adults have experience with dogs, but many children do not. Before bringing the Bernedoodle home, give your children instructions for how dogs are supposed to be treated. Emphasize the need to be gentle with the dog and to give it plenty of space. Let them know that if a dog growls at them, they need to stop whatever they were doing and back away.

Remember that children should always be supervised with dogs. It doesn't take much for something to go wrong during playtime and your dog to snap at your child. When stressed, even good dogs are capable of injuring children. A bad experience between your child and your Bernedoodle can leave a lasting impression on your family.

Dogs can get annoyed by children because they have a ton of energy and may not recognize a dog's cues that they're overstimulated. While you may notice that a tail between the legs means your dog is unhappy, your young child might not. Like any kind of socialization, your dog needs plenty of time and space to become comfortable. Luckily, this breed is typically very gentle with children.

Good socialization can change the way your dog sees the world. A socialized dog is a pleasure to be around and is happy and healthy. The owner benefits from a socialized Bernedoodle, too, because you can feel comfortable letting others care for your dog. Start early, and in no time, your Bernedoodle will feel comfortable with both people and other animals.

CHAPTER 8

BERNEDOODLES AND YOUR OTHER PETS

❝ *Bernedoodles have a very easy going nature. Typically any issue would arise with an older, jealous dog. Introduction should be slow and supervised at all times."*

Diane Caldemeyer-Reid
www.vonfarawayfarms.com

In this chapter, we'll take a closer look at integrating your new Bernedoodle into your pet family. Bernedoodles are pretty easygoing as a breed, so while they might be shy at first, they should be quick to make new friends. However, it can be hard to predict how animals will react in new environments.

Adopting a Bernedoodle can have its advantages when introducing your new dog to your pets. If the shelter knows anything about the previous owner, they can share their Bernedoodle's behavioral traits. Also, these shelters are full of differ-

Photo Courtesy of Kim Montgomery
www.bmdfamilyfarms.com

ent kinds of animals, so employees can observe how their dogs react around other dogs and cats. When you're looking for a dog to adopt, most shelters should be able to tell you how the Bernedoodle acts around other animals. If you see the perfect Bernedoodle and they tell you that it doesn't get along with other animals, resist the temptation to bring it home—it can be hard to change the animal's behavior and it will result in a lot of stress for your already established pets. On the other hand, an adopted dog may already be well-socialized and ready to meet your pets.

If you're purchasing a puppy from a breeder, there's still a little uncertainty in how it will react to other animals. It will be used to being around other dogs, but it's different when the other dogs are its mom and siblings. A well-bred dog should have a nice, even temperament, but it can be hard to account for chance. However, as long as the parents are good around people and other animals, it's more likely that the pups will be too.

Introducing Your New Puppy

As discussed in the last chapter, adding a new dog to your home takes a lot of time and patience. Instead of bringing your Bernedoodle home to meet its new sibling, find a neutral territory for their meeting. Your other dog may have feelings of ownership attached to the house and this can taint their first interaction. It helps to have a family member or friend help you with this first interaction. Keep both dogs on leashes so they can see and smell each other without getting too close.

Next, give them a large space to sniff each other out. This gives them the opportunity to play for a while without feeling too confined or trapped. If they get along, then you can proceed to letting them interact in your home. If they don't, give them plenty of space and try again later.

Once you have both dogs at home, let them interact outside where there are fewer possessions to feel territorial about. If they handle it well, let them interact inside the home. Keep their interactions as calm and positive as possible. If you're nervous and jumpy, your dogs might be able to pick up on that. Make sure they have ample space to interact in and take breaks often.

If you have other dogs in your home, talk to your breeder or animal shelter about taking the Bernedoodle home for a test run with the others. Sometimes, dogs are incompatible and forcing two unhappy dogs to live in close quarters can be dangerous.

Introducing your Bernedoodle to a cat may take a little more time. Make sure that each animal has its own space that the other cannot get to. If a cat gets cornered by your Bernedoodle, it is likely to go on the defensive. Your dog may be fascinated by your cat and want to check it out. In return, your cat might not be pleased with this.

Once your animals have gotten used to the idea of living under the same roof, it is time to let them interact under close supervision. Keep your dog on a leash and have someone close to your cat. Don't expect the dog and cat to play during this time. Instead, you want to see the animals become comfortable around one another, to the point where they are relaxed and can ignore each other.

Once you get to the point where they aren't bothered by each other, let them interact without close supervision. This should only be done if they have proven to you that they can co-exist without hurting each other.

Unfortunately, a cat might trigger a Bernedoodle's prey drive. If your dog cannot be distracted while the cat is in the room, or lunges at it, they might not be a good fit. If you do not have enough room for your pets to be separated, they may become agitated. If after a few months the dog and cat still can't get along while being supervised, then the match might not work out.

If your current pets aren't socialized, it might be a good idea to put your plans to bring a new dog into the family on hold. Give them some time to interact with different dogs. This will also help you decide if your current dog or cat can be trusted around a new dog. If you find that your animals are just not compatible with any dogs, it will save you heartbreak in the future when things don't work out.

Pack Mentality

Dogs are highly social creatures. They need other dogs, or humans, to spend time with. In the wild, dogs form close packs and take on roles within the pack. There is a leader who controls the pack and shows dominance. From there, the hierarchy continues to the bottom of the ranks to the most submissive. The alpha dog is in charge of leading the pack to ensure they survive. The other dogs must follow the alpha and obey its rules.

With domesticated dogs, the pack rules aren't as strict. Your dogs aren't out in the wild hunting for their food, so their pack instinct may not be as strong as their ancestors'. In fact, as your dogs' caretaker, your dogs may even view you or a member of your family as the alpha dog in their pack.

Bernedoodles are likely to form close relationships with others. They do best when they have plenty of attention and don't like to spend time alone. Their tendency to form a pack makes them especially protective of their human family. So, in a home with other dogs, your new Bernedoodle may be eager to join the ranks.

The hierarchy of the pack can be characterized by shows of dominance and submission. However, this is not a static role that dogs take on for life. In fact, it has been observed that dogs can show dominance in some situations and submission in others.

Photo Courtesy of Charlene Waggert

Shows of dominance or submission don't necessarily mean that anything is wrong with the dog. A dominant dog isn't necessarily aggressive, just like a submissive dog isn't necessarily fearful or anxious. When your pack interacts with each other, watch for signs of aggression, like growling and fighting. With a submissive dog, watch for signs of anxiety like nervous urination, putting its tail between its legs, and excessive panting.

The concept of a pack mentality is somewhat controversial between dog owners and experts. While it is widely acknowledged that dogs live in packs, it is not a steadfast rule. Different canine species and feral dogs have been observed to be somewhat social, but they do not fit into the alpha-beta hierarchy. Dogs aren't necessarily born into a certain spot in the ranks without any ability to change their position.

Your Bernedoodle's rank (or lack of one) in its pack does not have to affect its quality of life in any way. The only time it may become an issue is if one dog is aggressive towards another. But, as long as every dog is getting along, there's no need to try to change their order. You might find that one dog is the ringleader and the others are followers. This is perfectly normal.

At any rate, the dominant pup should not outrank the owner. As the leader, you are responsible for correcting bad behavior, just like an alpha dog would do in the wild. Lead with kindness and correct behavior with positive reinforcement and your dogs will respect your command.

Photo Courtesy of Marva Smith

Fighting

Sometimes, a dog's aggression goes a little too far. If you're planning on raising multiple dogs in your home, it's a good idea to know what to do in case of a fight. Many households don't have any issues with dogs fighting, but it's best to know what do to in the event of a fight, just in case.

If you notice that your Bernedoodle puppy is biting at another dog, this doesn't necessarily mean that they are fighting. Most of the time, your dogs will put their mouths on each other in play or to communicate. Generally, this kind of behavior does not hurt the dog.

Puppies use their mouths to check out their surroundings. That's why it's common for young dogs to nibble on your fingers or chew your belongings. They are using their bite to investigate the world around them. When dogs play, they learn how to control how hard they bite. If a dog gets too carried away and bites too hard, the other dog will yelp in pain. This sends a signal to the dog that it made a mistake. It will learn that biting too hard causes pain and makes dogs (and people) not want to play with it.

Fighting looks different from rough play. When a dog is gearing up to fight, its body becomes tense, it bares its teeth, and it will probably growl. It will also stare intensely at its target. If you see these signs of an imminent fight, try to command your dog to sit or lie down. This will hopefully give it enough time to cool down.

It can be stressful to see your dogs fighting, but it's important not to panic. Your dogs will sense your panic and may associate the sight of other dogs with fear or punishment. Try to get your dogs distracted enough so they divert their eye contact before the fight escalates.

Once a fight has begun, it needs to be stopped before serious injury occurs. However, it can be dangerous to try to get in between two fighting dogs. If you try to stand in the middle or grab them by the head or neck, they might mistake you for another dog and attack.

One method for breaking up a dog fight is to grab the dog by the back legs and pull it backwards away from the other dog. Let go quickly, or else the dog might turn around and bite you. Whatever you do, avoid putting your hands anywhere near the dogs' mouths. They will not recognize that you are trying to help and may even see it as a threat.

When dogs fight, it is because they feel threatened and afraid. A lot of fears can be eased by a calm owner. When dogs sense that their owner is concerned, it reinforces their thought that they might be in danger. Let your dogs know that you are the leader of the pack and that they must answer to you. In the meantime, good socialization skills will give your dogs the confidence they need around other dogs.

Raising Multiple Puppies

When choosing a new Bernedoodle, it might be hard to stop at just one. You may have decided that your want to have multiple dogs, or you want your new dog to have a companion. Before bringing home two puppies, decide if you have the time and energy for raising multiple puppies.

Taking care of just one puppy can be exhausting. They require so much care and training before they reach adulthood. Adding another puppy amplifies the amount of work you have to do. You can't expect each dog to be a carbon copy of the other, either. The puppies might have completely different personalities and different needs. It's quite possible that each dog will need more work in one area of training than the other.

Another concern is how the dogs will interact with each other. One belief is that puppies raised together will acquire "littermate syndrome". This means that the puppies may form an unhealthy bond. In some cases, this leads to aggression and fighting, or severe separation issues. If your puppies are unable to be separated for any length of time, something as simple as a vet visit for one dog will lead to severe stress in your animals.

In some cases, puppies purchased together end up having to be re-homed because the owner is unable to properly raise two dogs at once. If the puppies have already formed a close bond, this can give them separation anxiety. Anxious pups can display poor behaviors, like destructive habits.

If you do decide that you want to bring more than one puppy home at once, make sure that you raise them as individuals. This means that they need separate kennels so they can have their own personal space. The puppies should also have one-on-one time with their owners without the other dog present. It is hard work, but it is possible to successfully raise two puppies at once.

Raising two puppies at once can be challenging. Owners wanting to bring multiple dogs into their home might consider training one before getting another. This way, the dogs can be close in age without having to do double the work. If you only have the time and energy to raise one dog, yet bring two into your home at once, both dogs will be receiving insufficient care. Before bringing multiple dogs home at the same time, be honest with yourself about how you can dedicate the necessary resources that multiple puppies require.

What to Do if Your Pets Don't Get Along

" *Bernedoodles are generally very friendly dogs that get along well with other dogs. If you do get a dog with a more dominant personality they may not get along well with another dominant dog so you always want to introduce new dogs before allowing them to play together just to make sure they get along well with one another."*

Carol Heller
www.highmesadoodles.com

It can be upsetting to see that your beloved pets aren't getting along. Sometimes, whether it's caused by their temperament, poor socialization, or other behavioral trauma that's occurred, pets can get upset in the presence of certain animals.

You may be tempted to separate your pets if they show aggressive or anxious behavior, but this won't solve the problem. Your Bernedoodle has a keen sense of smell, so it will know that there's another animal in the home. Because it cannot see or interact with it, this may cause it to become even more curious or obsessed.

If your Bernedoodle was part of a fight, don't let the fear of another fight cause you to act nervous around your animals. You may feel like you're protecting your dog by pulling on it when it gets near to another dog, but this behavior could confuse it. Other dogs might sense this weakness, making them even more likely to strike.

After several weeks of careful integration into your home, if your new dog has trouble getting along with your existing pets, try to examine the situation to see what the problem might be.

One possible explanation for this behavior is that your existing pets feel like they're not getting enough attention now that there's a new family member. Try not to completely separate your pets, but make sure they get plenty of one-on-one time with you. This may include going on a walk, going to the dog park, or just enjoying a game of fetch in the back yard. If you're bringing in a new pet, make sure you can dedicate the same amount of time you used to spend with the pets you already have.

Another way to allow your pets to have their own space is by giving them their own crates. When trained correctly, a dog will use its crate as a safe nook to have a little alone time. If a dog feels anxious, it can relax in its crate, giving it time to cool down without being bothered by other animals. When dogs fight, it's because they're stressed out and are looking for a solution to their fear.

Sometimes, owners are unable to fix conflict between pets. If an animal is dangerously aggressive towards the others, it may need to be removed from the home if socialization and training fall short. No one wants to re-home an animal, so that is why early, gradual introductions are so important. Never force your pets to get along. This will only cause more stress. Dogs can be unpredictable at times because they communicate in ways that humans don't quite understand. They exchange so much information between each other just through subtle body language. Sometimes, a dog will just decide that it doesn't like another one within the first few minutes of meeting. These relationships may be improved by behavioral modification, but that might not always be available to you.

The key to getting your old and new pets to get along is to spend the necessary time and effort in introducing them to one another. If owners don't have the patience for meeting on neutral territory or supervising interactions, they can't expect their dogs to get along. Well-socialized pets, plus a slow and planned introduction, can make all the difference in your Bernedoodle's first few weeks at home. Talk to your breeder or animal shelter about bringing your Bernedoodle home for a trial run to ensure that all of your pets will be happy and safe during this exciting time.

Photo Courtesy of Thomas Lyford

CHAPTER 9

TRAINING YOUR BERNEDOODLE

Photo Courtesy of Carol Heller
www.highmesadoodles.com

66 *Because the Bernedoodles are so cute, folks tend to spoil them. I always tell my folks not to let their pups go at life with their mouth wide open. That little pup will be a big dog soon. Nip the bad habits in the bud early on and you will have an amazing companion for life!"*

Diane Caldemeyer-Reid
www.vonfarawayfarms.com
location: Chapter 9

Luckily for Bernedoodle owners, Bernedoodles are smart dogs, so training this breed should be a breeze! Depending on where your new dog is in life, this training stage will vary. An adult Bernedoodle from a shelter will likely already know a few tricks, so training will consist of building on prior knowledge or correcting bad habits. Training a young puppy will require an introduction to the basics, but will be like working with a fresh canvas. Remember that a Bernedoodle's mental maturation takes a little longer than other breeds, so practice is key. Once its brain develops more, it'll start picking things up more quickly.

Regardless of where your dog is in the training process or what commands you plan to teach your pup, the basics are the same. Training should always be relaxed and positive. Negativity and punishments will only upset your Bernedoodle and can jeopardize your training. Dogs don't have memories that function in the same was as humans do, so when trying to understand your dog's thought processes, think like a dog! Your Bernedoodle is just looking to please you, so show it that you appreciate its hard work.

Getting Everyone on the Same Page

Depending on your plan for dog training, there might be several people involved in teaching your Bernedoodle new commands. Family members, roommates, and dog trainers may all spend time working with your dog. When multiple people are involved, there needs to be consistency.

Giving a dog a command works because it learns to associate a certain action with a specific word, not because it understands human language. For example, if you use the command "stop" when you want your dog to put down your personal belongings, but your partner uses "no" and your trainer uses "drop it", then your dog will probably become confused. A human child can understand that those words roughly mean the same thing, but a young pup can't make the connection. Once your dog becomes more experienced, it may be able to understand similar commands, but at first, it probably won't.

That's why it's necessary to communicate with everyone who will have a hand in training and raising your dog. Decide on which commands you'll be using, so there won't be any mix-ups. You may also decide on which commands you'll be focusing on to start. Having a roommate teach your Bernedoodle how to roll over can be a fun trick, but not necessarily helpful when you're just trying to get it leash trained.

While communicating training expectations, decide which behaviors you will and won't allow in your household. Your dog may get confused if one owner is rewarding it with praise for jumping on the couch, while the other owner discourages it. These expectations are best discussed before your dog even comes home so you can start out without any confusion.

When everyone knows what's going on in your dog's training routine, they can work as a team. This way, you'll be working at maximum efficiency and no one will be negating anyone else's efforts. The lack of confusion will keep your dog stress-free and confident, which in turn will make it more eager to learn new commands.

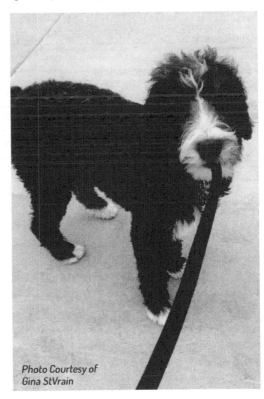

Photo Courtesy of Gina StVrain

Photo Courtesy of Carol Heller
www.highmesadoodles.com

Operant Conditioning Basics

Perhaps one of the most common techniques used for teaching dogs is operant conditioning. This term refers to B. F. Skinner's theory of how humans and animals respond to consequences of our behavior. The theory of operant conditioning is based on the voluntary choices we make in response to our surroundings. Instead of reacting to a stimulus, this theory is about displaying a certain behavior first, and discovering the consequences, good or bad.

In life, we face consequences for our behavior, especially as children. When a child receives a gold star from a teacher for doing well in school, it's seen as a reward for hard work. After enough gold stars, the child might continue to strive to achieve good grades, even if the rewards aren't still forthcoming. The child will associate good grades with the pride of receiving a positive response and connect the two in future work.

This applies to negative outcomes as well. Suppose the child failed an assignment. The teacher shows disapproval by not handing out a gold star, but also by assigning a punishment, like having to miss recess. After enough missed recesses, the child will learn to associate bad grades with feeling left out or deprived.

Skinner believed that by creating positive and negative outcomes for behavior, any behavioral trait could be modified using this system. Animals, like rats, were tested in such experiments by placing them in a box with no outside distractions. If the rats pressed one lever, they would be rewarded with a treat. If they pressed the other lever, they would be punished with a shock. Scientists found that the rats would eventually learn through the series of treats and shocks which lever to press and which one to avoid.

These conditioning theories are still used in dog training today. When training dogs, we wait for them to act. If we like how they behave, they receive a treat. They learn to associate certain behaviors with the rewards until the behavior becomes hardwired into their brains. It is also possible to train animals with punishments, but it has adverse effects on your pet and should be avoided.

Operant conditioning can also be used alongside classical conditioning. Classical conditioning is when a stimulus produces a result. The most well-known example of this was Pavlov's dog experiment. In this experiment, he fed dogs while ringing a bell. The food caused the dogs to salivate, but eventually, it only took the sound of the bell to cause salivation. The reaction to the stimulus is subconscious and involuntary. Both operant and classical training will cause a dog to learn commands, but one causes a purposeful reaction and the other causes an involuntary habitual reaction.

Primary Reinforcements

Once your dog has displayed the desired behavior, it needs to be rewarded. Rewards are a type of positive reinforcement. Primary reinforcements are rewards that have value in and of themselves. For dogs, the biggest primary reinforcements are food and play time.

Primary reinforcements don't need to be given every time the dog completes a task. Frequent rewards are good at first, because it helps your dog make a connection between your command and its behavior. Once it gets the hang of it, you can space your rewards out a little more.

In psychology, this is known as reinforcement schedules. If your dog knows the command, it won't stop doing it, just because it didn't get a dog treat one time. It will continue to do what you tell it to because it knows that one of the times it sits, it'll get a reward. It's random and unpredictable, but it still believes the good behavior will lead to a reward at some point.

Some trainers believe that using these types of reinforcement schedules are more effective than giving your dog a treat every time it performs. Think of this method as a slot machine—people become addicted to pulling the lever even though they don't get a reward every time. However, they believe that if they pull the lever enough times, it will pay out in a big way. This same theory applies to dogs as well. They'll keep performing the task with hopes that it will pay off.

Most pet owners will find that they can get their Bernedoodle to do just about anything for a tasty treat. These are a staple for training a new dog. When your dog receives a treat, its brain sends signals that makes it feel good. Since it is happy, it will associate whatever action that lead to the treat as a good thing to do.

Photo Courtesy of Cheryl Ziegler

Try to keep in mind how many dog treats your dog is eating over a training session. Your dog's nutrition comes from its daily meals, and its daily caloric intake is factored into that. Too many treats over a long period of time can cause weight gain, because your Bernedoodle is ingesting more calories than it requires.

This doesn't mean that it shouldn't get treats every now and again, but make sure not to overdo it. Instead of giving your dog a full biscuit every time it sits down, break one up into several small pieces, or use tiny treats. People food is generally not good for dogs, but some owners like to use fruits and vegetables for healthy training treats. Foods like berries, leafy greens and steamed sweet potatoes are full of nutrients and low in calories. Before feeding your dog anything that isn't manufactured specifically for pups, check with a vet to make sure that your dog will be able to digest it without any adverse effects.

Play time is also another reward that dogs love. This is a good reward for learning new skills like potty training. If your Bernedoodle manages to make it to the bathroom spot in the yard without any accidents, this deserves a reward. Instead of loading it up with more food, you can take it on a walk or throw a toy around.

This reward is also good to use on a random schedule because going on a walk after every potty break might be excessive, especially in small pups that go often. You can even alternate between tasty treats and play time for rewards. Your dog will be happy and it might even keep it from meandering around the yard when you let it out, because it knows that it will still have some time to play outside once it's finished.

Secondary Reinforcements

Secondary reinforcements are rewards that are associated with value, but don't necessarily have value in themselves. For example, humans are highly motivated by money. Money is just fancy paper, but humans have given it value. We can use the secondary reinforcement to trade it in for what we really want.

For dogs, this concept is a little trickier. But, there are some ways of rewarding dogs that don't necessarily have any intrinsic value. For instance, a pat on the head signals to your dog that it is loved. It knows this because when you pet and cuddle it, it can sense from your body language that you love it. It's safe to say that negative emotions won't get caught up in this, because people are less inclined to give their dog a belly rub after realizing that their dog destroyed their pillows. The words "good dog" and a pat on the head are connected to something it values: love.

That is why affection is a good motivator. Bernedoodles are sensitive dogs that aim to please. When you show them that you're happy with them in a language they can understand, they respond positively. This type of reward works well with this breed once they understand that praise means that their human is happy.

Another form of secondary reinforcement is clicker training. A clicker is a small device that emits a clicking sound whenever the button is pressed. The clicker in itself is not a reward, until the sound of the click is associated with a primary reinforcement, like a treat.

To begin clicker training your dog, you must teach it that the click signals a reward, like a dog treat. Once it understands that the sound of the click is linked to tasty dog treats, the click becomes the reward. Enough clicks can be "traded in" for another treat in the future.

One benefit of clicker training is that it is a precise way to communicate your idea of good behavior to your dog. For example, if by chance, your dog is calm when the doorbell rings instead of going wild, you can point out and reward its behavior in one short click. If the dog makes it outside before going to the bathroom, this gets a click.

Sometimes, giving a treat can be an imprecise reward system. If you're in the beginning stages of training and you command your dog to stay, it may only be able to remain motionless for a few seconds. If it gets up, it doesn't mean that it didn't perform the task at all, but giving a treat after it didn't entirely follow your command might send mixed signals.

With the clicker, you can give a click the moment you observe correct behavior because the reward can be delivered instantly. Once the training session is over, the dog can receive more rewards in exchange for clicks.

Clicker training has become popular with dog trainers because it is efficient at pointing out good behavior immediately. It also reduces the need for lots of dog treats, which may cause weight gain if used too frequently. The clicker approach is beneficial for owners who plan on doing a lot of training with their dog.

The Dangers of Punishment

66 *Since a Bernedoodle is a cross between two different breeds, they can be a little challenging to train as a young puppy. The Bernese is known to sometimes be a bit headstrong and stubborn, and Poodles can be very high energy and are very intelligent. This can make for a difficult combination during early puppy training. "*

Brian Montgomery
www.bmdfamilyfarms.com

In operant conditioning, punishment is the opposite of reward. There are two types: positive punishment and negative reward. A positive punishment is something we receive as a consequence for our actions. For example, a child receives a spanking for misbehaving. The child misbehaved, so in response, he or she received something that they did not want.

A negative reward is the removal of something that we do want. If a child misbehaves, the parent might take away television privileges. The parent will withhold something the child wants instead of giving something the child doesn't want.

With dogs, the type of "punishment" they receive matters. If your dog is constantly barking at your front window, this isn't a behavior that deserves to be rewarded. It may enjoy looking out the window at everyone who walks by, but its constant barking is annoying. In response, you may decide to put it in a less fascinating room without windows until it calms down. In operant conditioning, this would be regarded as a punishment because you're withholding something the dog wants because of bad behavior.

However, this is much different than positive punishment. Common forms of positive punishment involve pain, like swatting or spanking, or fear, like screaming and yelling. Punishment does change behaviors, but not always in the way that you want.

For example, someone might catch their Bernedoodle digging a hole into the leather sofa. In anger, they lash out at the dog and hit it to teach it a lesson. The highly sensitive Bernedoodle will become upset. It may even fear its owners and will avoid them whenever they are near. The stressed out Bernedoodle is then less likely to learn new commands because it's afraid its owner is going to hurt it again.

Also, it may decide that its owners were angry because they caught it destroying something. With this new fear of getting caught again, it may hide when it feels like being destructive.

Punishments will likely change your dog's behavior in one way or another, but at risk to its safety and the safety of others. As discussed in the socialization chapter, fearful, anxious dogs are more likely to lash out at others for protection. The stress hormones are not good for the dog and fear leads to aggression. For this reason, punishment should be avoided at all costs.

This is not to say that dogs should be allowed to display bad behavior in front of you. However, a deterrent or distraction is much more effective than a punishment. Try to get your dog's attention without being overly forceful. Your Bernedoodle can probably tell the difference between a shout and a firm command. Some sounds, like clapping one's hands or shaking a jar full of rocks might be enough to grab its attention. You can even give a firm, but kind, "no" or "hey". This should get its attention so you can correct its behavior.

It is also important to remember that your dog cannot be corrected unless you are witnessing the behavior. A dog will not remember something it did a half hour ago, so it won't be able to comprehend being scolded for it. Showing it the mess it made won't jog its memory, either. You may think that it is showing signs of feeling ashamed when you return home to a mess, but it's more likely that it senses your anger and is scared.

Dog training is tough work and it can be easy to lose your cool when you're trying to teach your dog how to behave in the home. If you find yourself becoming frustrated, take a step back and try again later. Training should be a fun and exciting time

Photo Courtesy of Maggie Box
www.angelviewdoodles.com

for both you and your dog. Dog training is all about forming the right connections in your dog's mind, so making it feel happy and confident will only make your job easier.

Professional Dog Training

Dog training is a lot of hard work, so don't feel like you have to go through it alone. Especially if you don't have a lot of experience working with dogs, working with a trainer can be extremely helpful. A good trainer is also invaluable when working with a dog that has behavioral problems that are too much for you to handle alone.

The first step is to find a good dog trainer. This is not a profession that requires any certain degrees or qualifications, so you'll want to do your research. The prospective trainer should be happy to talk to you and share his or her qualifications. It's important to find a trainer that you get along with because you'll be spending time together and trusting them to cater to your dog's needs.

Some trainers use controversial training techniques that may not be best for your dog's wellbeing. Ask them about the methods they use when they train. You'll want to make sure they stress the importance of positive training techniques. Anything having to do with pack dominance, yelling, or getting physical with your dog should send up red flags for you.

Next, choose what kind of class you want to enroll in. Trainers often offer private classes, group classes, and training where the owner is not present. Choose the type that best fits in with your lifestyle and schedule. Group classes can be highly beneficial because they add in the socialization aspect. For dogs that don't have a lot of experience around other dogs or people, this is a great way to make them feel more comfortable around others in a safe setting.

Finally, check if your trainer offers different classes for different stages of life. Puppies may require different techniques and concentrations as opposed to adult dogs. You'll also want to enroll your new dog in a class for beginners so you won't get frustrated by having to learn advanced commands before mastering the basics.

Once you find a trainer that you're interested in, ask for client referrals. A reputable dog trainer should be happy to give you all the information you need. Ask past or current clients if they enjoy their training sessions and if their dogs are getting something out of it. A vet or breeder is also a good source of information when it comes to finding the right trainer.

Dog training can be a fun way to spend time with your new Bernedoodle. Once your dog learns a few commands, it will be happier and more entertained because it needs to feel like it has a specific job to do. A physically and mentally stimulated Bernedoodle is less likely to get itself into boredom-related trouble. Dog training takes a lot of time and effort, but the end result is a happy pup and a happy owner.

CHAPTER 10

BASIC COMMANDS

❝ *Bernedoodles are not low maintenance dogs, and are going to require a lot of time and effort to become properly trained and socialized dogs. Owners should be prepared to work with their puppy, especially the first few years to provide training, exercise, and attention and love. "*

Brian Montgomery
www.bmdfamilyfarms.com

Photo Courtesy of Jean Etzel

Now that you understand how your dog learns new skills, it's time to put that knowledge into practice. While there is no limit to the amount of fun tricks you can teach your dog, there are some commands that are necessary for your dog's wellbeing. Whether you're training your dog on your own or with help from a professional, this chapter will cover the basics of commands that are important for Bernedoodles to learn.

Benefits of Proper Training

A well-trained dog is safer than an untrained dog because dogs don't always understand the dangers of the human world. For example, if your dog likes to run outside the second the door opens, it might be too excited to watch for cars driving down the street. In this situation, simply teaching it to sit on command gives you some control over your dog's actions.

A well-trained dog can also make your life easier. When you spot your Bernedoodle walking around with your shoe, it's much more productive to give the command to drop it than it is to chase the dog around to snag the shoe from its mouth.

These skills can also make other dogs and people feel comfortable around your Bernedoodle. Some people and dogs are nervous around energetic dogs, so an eager pup might make them a little uneasy. If you can teach your dog to sit or lie down in exciting situations, it will make others feel more comfortable around your Bernedoodle.

Basic Commands

There are tons of different commands for dogs to learn. However, as an owner, you must ask yourself if you have the time and energy to commit your days to teaching your Bernedoodle how to perform certain tasks. Regardless of your intentions with training, there are some skills that should not be skipped. Once your dog learns the basics, then you can continue with more advanced or fun commands.

When working on your commands, go to a quiet place with no distractions. Your puppy is probably still fascinated by its surroundings so keep outside factors to a minimum to start.

Sit

This is perhaps the most common command taught to dogs. The "sit" command can protect your dog from danger, while also protecting others from your enthusiastic pup. Having it sit when it gets overexcited will also help calm it down. When the dog sits, it is implied that it should stay in the seated position until you give another command. The Bernedoodle should wait attentively for the next command.

To teach the "sit" command, take a treat and raise it just above the dog's head. When its head goes up, the dog should automatically go down into the seated position. If it has a hard time figuring this out, you may also want to place a hand on its bottom and gently apply pressure downward. Give the command, and then give the reward once it is seated. Keep practicing this motion until your dog can do it without the treats. Because you'll be practicing this command often, try giving a treat at random intervals.

Photo Courtesy of Maggie Box
www.angelviewdoodles.com

Photo Courtesy of Maggie Box
www.angelviewdoodles.com

Lie Down

"Lie down" is the next natural command to learn after "sit" is mastered. This command is useful for keeping your dog still and in control. This position takes more effort to get out of than a sitting position so it's good to use when you need your Bernedoodle to stay still for a little longer. It can also be a comfortable position to hang out in, so it's useful for getting your dog to chill out before bedtime.

To start out, have your dog begin in a seated position. Hold the dog treat in front of your dog's nose and slowly move it to the ground, Your dog should want to follow the movement of your hand. Once your hand gets to the floor, use your hand to cover the treat so it can't be snatched from your fingers. When the dog gets into the correct position, praise it and give the treat. If the dog stands up to get the treat, try to hold the treat closer to its body. If you lure it too far forward, it may scoot forward to get the treat.

Before starting, decide what command you plan on using for this motion. Many owners use "down" for this position, but it can be confusing if you also plan on using "down" when you want your dog to stop jumping on people or objects.

Stay

Once your dog is in a seated or down position, it may need to be instructed to stay put for a little while. While you may eventually teach your dog that "sit" and "lie down" also include staying still until you give a new command, the "stay" command is a good way to practice being motionless.

This command is useful when you need your dog to sit or lie down, and you need to emphasize that it needs to stay put for a moment. It's good for an active dog that needs to be able to relax when it gets overstimulated. It's also a good skill for your dog to have when you have to divert your attention from your dog and you need to be able to trust it to behave.

To teach this command, start with commanding your dog to sit or lie down. Once it's ready, give the "stay" command while holding your hand like a stop sign in front of its nose. If it can hold the position for a few seconds, give a reward. Over time, practice holding the position for longer intervals of time. At first, stay close to your dog, but then slowly add distance between you and your dog to make things more challenging.

Come

This is another skill that can protect your dog from dangerous situations. If you see your curious dog running away from you to go exploring, it's important to be able to retrieve it with a simple command. When you call your dog, always meet it with praise when it comes to you. If you call your dog with the intent to punish it, it will learn that it doesn't like to come to you and won't feel like it's being rewarded.

Teach your dog the "sit" and "stay" commands first because the "come" command will build on past training. When beginning, keep your dog on a leash and have it sit and stay. Walk to the end of the leash and call it to come. Your voice should be inviting and positive, but not high-pitched and frantic. If your dog does not come to you, gently tug on the leash to prompt it. This isn't meant to correct it, but to give a hint about what you want from it. Once it comes to you, have it sit at your feet and reward it. When your dog starts to get it, create more distance and practice the command again. When taught correctly, your dog should drop everything to come to you.

Off

There is a good chance that an excited Bernedoodle pup will want to jump up on people and things. While this might seem cute at first, after a while it can be irritating. Plus, your Bernedoodle will grow to be quite large, and your dog jumping on a small child could knock them right over. This command requires consistency among people interacting with your dog. Once you teach your dog not to jump on people, it should not be encouraged to jump only on certain people. Some may see it as a sign of affection from the dog and want to encourage it. If you decide you don't want to allow your dog to jump on people, make it a household rule.

Depending on the rules you've set for your dog, you may not want it to jump up on your furniture. Even if you allow your dog to sit on the couch or bed, you still may want a command in case your Bernedoodle puts its paws on your kitchen table to grab a snack. If you're teaching your dog that furniture is off limits, stay consistent with that rule. A dog might not be able to tell the difference between your new, white sofas that are off limits and your old recliner that is an acceptable place for them to sit.

Some owners will opt to call this command "down" but keep in mind that it can cause confusion. If you're using "down" for lie down, your dog might do a completely different action. "Off" works well because there's a good chance you won't use that word for another command.

This command might be trickier than the others to teach because it requires your dog to jump up on you to create the teaching moment. Young dogs will probably be keen to jump on people, so before long, you'll be able to anticipate your Bernedoodle's next move.

When your dog jumps, turn your back and show it that you aren't going to give it any attention when it acts that way. Give the "off" command. When it jumps down, give it a treat. Another method is to keep its leash connected at a time when it is likely to jump. Place your foot on the leash, making it physically impossible to jump up. When it obeys your command, reward it.

If your dog likes to jump on furniture, give the "off" command and hold a treat on the ground. Once it gets down, give it the treat. Whether your dog is on your furniture or has its front paws on your shirt, never pet it or give it attention. Once it learns that you won't engage with it in the way it wants, it will stop trying.

Drop It

Photo Courtesy of Charlene Waggert

This command is useful in a few different situations. It can be helpful if you have a curious Bernedoodle that likes to claim your objects as its own. It can also save your dog's life if you catch it nosing around something hazardous to its health. For instance, if you catch your dog picking up a chocolate bar from your table, you need a sure-fire way to keep the dog from eating it.

To teach the "drop it" command, give your dog its favorite toy to play with. Next, hold a dog treat in front of your dog's face and give the "drop it" command. Your dog will probably be more interested in the treat than the toy, so it will drop the toy in favor of the treat. Once the dog drops the toy, give it the treat. As your dog becomes better at this command, let it practice in a place with more distractions. You want to get to the point where your dog is willing to drop whatever tasty thing it might find on your command.

Leash Training

When you take your dog out on its leash, you want to walk the dog, not the other way around. This breed has a lot of energy, so they require lots of walks. For its safety and your sanity, you'll want your dog to be on its best behavior during your daily exercise. When your dog is heeling, or walking by your side, your dog should be on the left side of you. Your dog should be walking close to you with its head in line with your leg. If it surges ahead or lags behind, it needs to be corrected.

This can take a lot of practice, since many dogs get excited and like to run ahead and pull on the leash. Bring some treats along with you on a walk, and practice giving the "heel" command and having your dog walk with you. Hold the leash close, so your dog won't have any leash to pull.

Photo Courtesy of Jean Etzel

Start off by slowly walking a few steps together, then stop and command your dog to sit. Once you can get it to walk a few steps beside you before sitting, then extend the number of steps you take. After enough stop and go, your dog will learn that it is supposed to stay near. Whatever you do, don't allow your dog to pull you. If it tries, turn around and walk in the other direction.

Advanced Commands

Once you master these basic commands, it's time to challenge your Bernedoodle with new commands. If your dog has something new to learn, it's more likely to feel entertained enough to stay out of trouble. Many advanced commands just build on basic commands, so by the time you're ready for the harder stuff, half the work is already done. Here are a few ideas of commands to teach your Bernedoodle once the basics are covered.

Fetch

This trick will make your playtime more fun. Your Bernedoodle will think it is performing an important job, and it will give you two something to do together. If it gets good enough at it, you might even trust your dog to fetch certain items for you.

For this command, start with a toy and find a quiet place to practice. Throw the toy and get the dog to retrieve it. If it drops the toy at your feet, reward it. It will need to use its skills from the "drop" command. Then, it gets the food reward and the chance to play again.

Shake

This trick doesn't necessarily serve a larger purpose in the wellbeing of your dog, but it's a fun trick to show your friends. If your dog can sit at attention around strangers for long enough to shake, then it probably won't be liable to jump up or bark at your guests.

To teach this command, have your dog start in a seated position. Hold a dog treat in your closed fist. Give the "shake" command and hold your fist in front of the dog. It will probably raise its paw to investigate the hidden object in your hand. When it does the shake motion, give it the treat. This trick is pretty simple for novice trainers, but fun to teach your dog.

Take It

If your dog has mastered the "drop it" command, the next step is to teach it to pick something up. This command can be used for a variety of purposes, from starting a game of fetch to teaching your dog to put its toys away.

To start, place your dog's favorite toy in front of it. Give the "take it" command and wait for it to naturally pick up the toy. When it succeeds, give it a treat. Once your dog masters "take it" and "drop it" try introducing the names of its toys or other household objects. Eventually, it may even be able to bring you an object by name.

Go

This command also requires the knowledge of the names of places. This can be a helpful command if you want to direct your dog somewhere without actually leading it there. For example, you could command "go backyard" or "go crate" to prompt your dog to go to a safe place. You might also try "go bed" at the end of the night. This can make things easier on the owner if their Bernedoodle gets too excited and needs a safe place to go.

While there are different ways to teach this command, perhaps the simplest one is to start with your dog seated in front of you. Give the "go to place" command and with a treat in hand, lure it to that place. Once it is seated or lying down in the place, give it the treat. Once your dog knows the names of the places, you will no longer need to guide it there. If it can make it to the place on its own, reward it with treats.

Training your new Bernedoodle may seem intimidating at first, but once you get going, you'll want to teach your dog all sorts of new tricks. Obedience training is an important part of your dog's development because it gives it the skills it needs to live in your home and keeps its mind happy. Bernedoodles are intelligent dogs that are eager to please. This breed wants to be able to "work" and show off their skills to the people that love them.

Photo Courtesy of Maggie Box

CHAPTER 11

NUTRITION

❝ *It is very important for a standard sized Bernedoodle to be on a large breed formula. Many large breeds, including the Bernedoodle, are prone to skeletal disorders (like hip dysplasia) and it is thought that excessive dietary calcium that occurs from overfeeding during the puppy phase of life can these conditions worse. ❞*

Brian Montgomery
www.bmdfamilyfarms.com

Proper nutrition should begin at an early age. Once the dog is weaned from its mother's nutrient-rich milk, it will begin eating man-made foods. Whether your dog will be chowing down on commercial dog food or a homemade blend, the owners have sole responsibility of the nutrients their dog consumes. It can be overwhelming to pick a dog food when there are so many on the market, but when you know what to look for in a food, it's easier to make a decision on what is best for your dog.

Importance of a Good Diet

A dog depends on its humans for food, and this includes the types of foods it's eating, how much food it's eating, and when the meal times take place. These variables require change throughout its life, so it is necessary to observe your dog's growth and development to know when something needs to be adjusted. Bernedoodles, like all dogs, are genetically predisposed to have certain health issues. A good diet can prevent some illness and injury and perhaps even extend the life of your dog.

An improper diet may exacerbate health conditions in your dog. Just like with people, eating unhealthy foods can make your dog feel sluggish and uncomfortable. As much as we may believe that dogs can eat everything (especially after you've watched them devour something yucky) they often have dietary intolerances or allergies. These things vary from dog to dog, so it's important to understand your dog's daily health so you know right away when something isn't quite right.

Bernedoodles are already big dogs, and any unnecessary weight is not good for their bodies. Having an extra-thick layer of fat around the internal organs causes them to work less efficiently than they would in a leaner dog. The extra pounds can also put a lot of pressure on bones and joints. Plus, your fluffy Bernedoodle may overheat faster on a hot day if it has an extra layer of fat on its body. It may be cute to have a chubby dog, but it can wreak havoc on its body.

Essential Nutrients

Big dogs have different nutritional requirements than small dogs. As a large breed, your Bernedoodle will need certain nutrients that aren't always found in your average small breed formula. While small dogs need a little extra protein in their food to keep their muscles healthy, large dogs need a little more carbohydrates to keep their energy up.

Carbohydrates should come from whole grain sources like brown rice, barley, and oats. Whole grains are good for dogs because the energy from them stays in the bloodstream longer than simple carbs do. Simple carbohydrates, like white rice,

Photo Courtesy of Steve Hetherington

Photo Courtesy of Steve Hetherington

are easy to digest, but only give a short burst of energy. Once your dog's blood sugar dips back down, it will be tired and hungry. Complex carbs also contain more fiber, which will make your dog feel full and aid in digestion.

There is some controversy about types of carbohydrates used when it comes to commercial dog food. Some owners are against feeding their dog "filler grains". Ingredients like corn, wheat, and soy are often referred to as "filler grains" because they provide a lot of calories and satiate your dog, but lack nutrients. Another reason these ingredients are often avoided is because many owners believe that these grains trigger an allergic response in dogs.

However, as long as your dog can tolerate these ingredients, there isn't any reason to cut them out of your dog's diet. Many dog foods contain both quick energy and slow releasing energy. If your dog appears to be exceptionally sluggish, itchy, has abnormal bowel movements, or appears to have stomach discomfort, then it might be time to try a new food.

Protein is another important part of your dog's diet. Dogs are meat-eaters, so make sure the dog food has at least 20% protein. Different types of meats can be found in dog food, from poultry, to red meats, to fish. Each type of protein has its advantages. Sometimes, a dog food will list meat "meal" in the ingredients, which can cause alarm in some dog owners. While meat meal is the term for a mix of different parts of the animal, including muscle, fat, and cartilage, this is not necessarily an inferior ingredient to just plain animal muscle. Both fat and animal cartilage are essential for your dog's health.

While humans might try to avoid animal fats in their diets, dogs need it for a variety of reasons. For dogs, animal fats are more useful than plant fats for dissolving the vitamins they need to stay healthy. Fat is also a good source of energy, when included in the right amounts. If a dog doesn't get enough fat in its diet, its skin and coat will look brittle and dry. Fats give dogs that healthy looking sheen to their coats. Fish oil is especially good for dogs because it contains Omega fatty acids. These fatty acids perform a number of roles in the body, from skin health to brain health.

Just like in our human diets, fruits and vegetables should not be excluded. While virtually all commercial dog foods contain vitamin and mineral supplements, real produce contains the nutrients they need. Fruits and vegetables also contain compounds that make it easier for your dog to absorb the nutrients better than it can from supplement mixes. Look for dog foods that contain a wide array of fruits and vegetables. Foods like leafy greens, berries, and sweet potato contain antioxidants, which may support many functions in the body, stave off disease, and promote longevity. While no nutritionist can promise you that your big dog will exceed its average lifespan by adding fruits and vegetables to its diet, it certainly can't hurt to try.

Joint problems are common in big dogs, so their diet needs to have the right levels of certain nutrients. Compounds like glucosamine and chondroitin are often added to dog foods because they are good for your dog's joints. These supplements work to protect your dog's joints and repair damage that has already been done. These ingredients are often found in dog food in the form of chicken cartilage or chicken meal. While it may sound gross that your dog's food contains animal cartilage, it's actually a good source of glucosamine and chondroitin.

Dog foods also frequently contain different types of fiber and probiotic supplements. These are added to foods to aid in your dog's digestion. Fiber is good for helping your dog feel satiated and promotes healthy bowel movements. However, too much fiber can cause excessive gas and abnormal bowel movements. Whole grains and fruits and vegetables are good, natural sources of fiber and can help keep your dog regular.

Adjusting for Different Life Stages

Some puppies can transition to adult food after about a year, and have no problem. But, because Bernedoodles are so big, their food intake and food quality is important in their formative years. Puppies take in a lot of calories, but Bernedoodle puppies are special. While they still need plenty of calories, if they have too many, they will grow too quickly. The same goes for calcium—if there's too much in the puppy food, the Bernedoodle's limbs will outgrow its joints. Bernedoodles develop slowly, so they may need to be on a puppy diet for longer than the average breed. Giant and large breed puppy food contains lower levels of calcium and a controlled number of calories per serving. When in doubt, talk to your breeders about what they feed their dogs.

Once you make the switch to adult food, there's less concern about your dog's growth. A dog food with normal levels of calcium should not be a concern. When feeding your Bernedoodle, it's necessary to use the feeding guidelines on the dog food package. The serving sizes go by your dog's weight, which tells you how many calories it can reasonably eat. Of course, if you find your Bernedoodle is particularly active (or inactive) you can add or subtract from the serving until you get the perfect amount to keep it at a healthy weight.

Once your Bernedoodle reaches an advanced age, it won't require as many calories as it did when it was young and active. A dog can put on a lot of weight if it isn't burning off the same amount of calories as it eats. Once it becomes less active, slowly cut back on the amount of food it gets in a day if weight gain is apparent.

Different Types of Commercial Food

With so many dog foods on the market, it can be hard to choose one. There are so many factors that come into play with dog food. A good place to start when looking for a new food is to talk to your breeder or vet about good options. However, you may find that the foods they recommend are expensive or are difficult for you to find where you live.

As long as your dog doesn't have any conditions that make it difficult for it to eat hard food, opt for a crunchy kibble over a soft, wet food. Canned foods contain liquid so your dog will be more interested in eating it. This is good for a picky dog or a pup with mouth problems. However, wet food isn't good for your dog's teeth. The soft chunks will stick on the teeth and cause plaque buildup if the dog doesn't find a way to scrape it off. Dry foods actually clean your dog's teeth as they chew, because the crunchy pieces of food scrape against the teeth, removing buildup.

Next, consider the quality of the dog food options. Now that you know what Bernedoodles need in their diet, you can look over ingredients lists and see if they match your dog's needs. While there isn't a lot of research done on the effects of certain ingredients in dog food, some owners like to avoid foods with artificial colors or flavors. Some owners also like foods that use local ingredients. While the use of certain ingredients like "filler grains" and animal by-products is often vilified among dog lovers, they can provide necessary nutrition. It's also not a bad idea to look for foods that use whole grains and real fruits and vegetables.

As much as all pet owners want to give their dogs the best of everything, some dog foods are very expensive. Also, remember that your big Bernedoodle will eat much more than a smaller breed. Over time, the cost of food adds up. You may decide that the fancy organic dog food is more than you can afford. There are still quality dog foods that are affordable. Read the ingredients and nutrition facts on the back of the dog food package, and depend less on the enticing buzz-words on the front.

Photo Courtesy of Diane Caldemeyer-Reid
www.vonfarawayfarms.com

Homemade Food

Some dog owners avoid commercial food altogether by giving their dogs homemade food. There can be both benefits and downfalls to giving your dog a food you create in your home.

On the plus side, when you make your own dog food, you'll know exactly what your dog is eating. With some commercial dog foods, it can be nearly impossible to trace where an ingredient came from and know the quality of it. With homemade dog foods, you might even be able to grow some of the ingredients in your own garden.

Another major benefit for making your own dog food is to help Bernedoodles with allergies or digestion issues. Every dog is different, and some dogs just can't eat the same ingredients as other dogs. There are some ingredients, like chicken, that pop up in most foods in some quantity. If your dog happens to have an intolerance to one or more of these foods, it can make buying commercial food difficult. When you make your own dog food, you can easily eliminate the problem ingredients.

On the down side, it can be hard to make your own dog food and most of the population does not have professional experience in dog nutrition. An inexperienced or undereducated owner may omit certain nutrients that can cause nutrient deficiencies in their dog.

Making your own dog food can also be expensive. Many ingredients in dog foods come from sources that were unable to sell their product for human consumption. This doesn't necessarily mean they are dangerous or inedible, but people can be picky about what their foods look like and prefer certain parts of the animal to others. Dog food companies can buy their ingredients in bulk. If you're cooking for your dog, you're probably limited to the ingredients in your local grocery store. For some owners, this is a plus—they don't want their dog to eat something they wouldn't want to eat. For other owners, they don't think their dog would have any problem eating an ugly, misshapen carrot.

If you do decide to make your dog's food, find a good recipe and stick to it. Do not leave out foods or make substitutions because you might unintentionally miss out on an important nutrient. Also, keep in mind that your dog is an animal and needs to eat certain foods. For example, an owner might be a vegan, but it is unfair and unhealthy to give the dog the same dietary restrictions. Food recipes should come from a veterinarian that has experience with nutrition.

People Food

While it may be hard to tell your dog "no" when it's eyeing your dinner, you should resist giving it a bite. Table scraps are not good for your dog for a variety of reasons. First, if you give your dog a taste of your food, it will feel like it is being rewarded for begging for food. You'll have to teach your dog that begging is unacceptable behavior. This can be confusing because it goes against what it has already learned. This is a behavior that you must be consistent with. You can't give your dog scraps from the table one day and deny them another.

Also, dogs get their nutrition through their dog food. Their portions are carefully calculated by their body weight. Adding more food to their diet can cause weight gain. This extra weight can put a lot of unnecessary strain on their organs and skeletal system.

Finally, some people foods just aren't good for dogs. Dogs aren't used to eating the same types of food that we are accustomed to, so your dinner might make your dog ill. Your dog may be able to digest its own food just fine, but your food might cause digestive troubles.

If you must feed people food to your dog, there need to be rules in place. Don't feed your dog scraps from the kitchen table or around your supper time. You can save leftovers to feed to your dog at its own meal time. Fruits and vegetables can also be used as training treats. Berries, leafy greens, and steamed sweet potatoes are good for dogs and can motivate them to obey your commands.

Photo Courtesy of Tanis Connors

There are some people foods that you should never feed your dog, regardless of the situation. Some foods can cause severe illness or even death in your pet. Before giving your dog people food, check with your vet to make sure your dog should be eating it and don't let others feed your dog. Here are a few common people foods that dogs should never eat:

Onions and garlic are seemingly healthy foods that can have dangerous effects if ingested by your dog. These foods cause anemia by breaking down red blood cells. Symptoms include vomiting, lethargy, weakness, lack of appetite, and shortness of breath. In tiny amounts, these foods won't necessarily cause serious problems. However, it is best to avoid them altogether. This also includes foods that contain onions and garlic.

Despite how tasty it is, chocolate is toxic to dogs. The compound found in all types of chocolate in varying amounts can cause illness, even in small amounts. Dogs will vomit and have diarrhea after eating chocolate. They may also display excessive thirst. If they do not get help immediately they may have a seizure, have abnormal heartbeat, or if they ingest enough, die.

Unlike chocolate, it isn't always common knowledge that grapes and raisins can be deadly for dogs because they seem like healthy treats. Soon after your dog eats grapes, it will start vomiting and lethargy will follow. Eventually, the grapes will lead to kidney failure.

Despite the fact that your dog loves to chew on nylon bones, it's not a good idea to give your dog leftover bones from your dinner. Some bones, like chicken bones, splinter easily when chewed and can easily get lodged in your dog's delicate digestive system. Instead of giving your dog scrap bones to chew on, give it ones that are specifically made for dogs.

Obesity and Dieting

Extra weight on your Bernedoodle's frame can be hazardous for its health. The best way to prevent unnecessary weight gain is to stick to the feeding guidelines on the bag of dog food and to give your dog plenty of exercise. In addition to play time, one nice, long walk every day is needed.

If you aren't sure if your dog is overweight, you can talk to your vet about the range your particular Bernedoodle should be in. It should be weighed at its regular checkup, so you can watch for changes in weight. Otherwise, one way to tell is to examine its frame. When your dog's fur is damp from a bath, look at it from above. There should be a clear waistline that tucks into its hips. If its body is a straight line from ribs to hips, it may have too much fat. You should also be able to feel the ribs under its skin, but not be able to see them.

If your dog is overweight, it is your responsibility to get your dog back into shape. Your dog needs to burn more calories than it eats. Adjust your Bernedoodle's exercise and diet until this occurs. Be careful not to work a sedentary dog too hard at first, or it might overheat or become exhausted.

Start by cutting extra dog treats out of the diet. If this isn't enough, slowly reduce the amount of food you feed it during daily meals. If your Bernedoodle whines for more, be tough and ignore it. You may feel like a cruel owner, but you're doing the best you can for your dog.

If cutting back on food and increasing exercise don't work, talk to your vet. Your dog might need to be put on a special diet or may even have an undiagnosed medical condition that makes it hard to shed the pounds.

Your dog's diet can potentially make or break its quality of life. When choosing a dog food, look for nutrients that Bernedoodles need to keep their weight in check and their joints healthy. Feed consistent amounts at regular intervals and avoid people food whenever possible. You may feel like you're being restrictive when it comes to food allowances, but you dog will appreciate feeling healthy and energetic.

Photo Courtesy of Jean Etzel

CHAPTER 12

GROOMING YOUR BERNEDOODLE

“ *Most Bernedoodles have a wavy coat that doesn't shed much if at all. This can be of great benefit to owners with allergies to dog dander, and while there are no guarantees, most will experience no allergies from a dog with a wavy coat. “*

Brian Montgomery
www.bmdfamilyfarms.com

Grooming your dog not only makes it look pretty, but is good for its health. Bernedoodles are beautiful dogs, so you'll want to keep yours at its very best. Some grooming tasks can be performed every couple of months, but some need to be done on a regular basis. Most things can be done at home, but you might want to hire out a groomer for some of the trickier work. At first, your pup might not know what to think of all of the primping and trimming, but if you start at an early age, it will learn that grooming is just part of its regular routine.

The Bernedoodle Coat

The Bernedoodle has a lovely, unique coat, thanks to its Bernese Mountain Dog and Poodle parents. A Bernese Mountain Dog's coat is thick and soft, but it sheds more than most breeds. A Poodle's coat is short and curly, and sheds very little. Combined, Bernedoodles can have a straight, wavy, or curly coat, depending on how they were bred.

Generally, the curlier the Bernedoodle's coat, the less it sheds. Its low shed coat is one reason why this crossbreed is so popular—it gives the lovable Bernese Mountain Dog a coat that doesn't constantly leave fur around your house.

However, if a breeder tells you that their Bernedoodles are hypo-allergenic and shed-free, you should be a little wary. No dogs are completely free of allergens or incapable of shedding a little fur. It is true that the Bernedoodle sheds far less fur than the Bernese Mountain Dog, but don't be surprised when you find a little fur on

Photo Courtesy of Alicia Marshall
"Highfalutin Furry Babies Bernedoodles"

the dog bed. Similarly, people with dog allergies will likely have less of a reaction to Bernedoodles, but it is still possible that interactions with this breed will cause an allergic reaction in some.

Poodle crossbreeds tend to require moderate maintenance in terms of grooming their coats, depending on the type. Curly coats are harder to take care of than wavy coats because curly coats need to be kept short in order to prevent matting.

A good diet can also help with the appearance of your dog's coat. Food with the right amount of fats gives the coat a smooth, shiny appearance. A dry, brittle coat may signal a nutrient deficiency or some other ailment. If your dog's coat is looking duller than normal or you've noticed any other symptoms, consult with your veterinarian.

Brushing and Bathing

Frequent brushing is very important for a Bernedoodle's coat health. The curlier the coat, the more easily it will become matted, making a painful mess for your dog. Because these dogs don't shed a lot, they need your help to remove their dead hair.

For this breed, look for a brush with thin, wire bristles. A brush that's made for matted fur will work well on a curly coat. When you brush, make sure you get the hairs below the surface, otherwise, the layer of hair next to the skin will become matted and you might not even be able to tell.

Bernedoodles need to be brushed at least every other day to keep their fur from becoming matted and to redistribute natural oils throughout the hair. Most dogs will enjoy being brushed because it should feel good, as long as their hair isn't being tugged at. If your dog is especially squirmy during this time, you may condition it to enjoy being brushed by giving it a treat after it's successfully sat through a brushing.

If the fur goes without being brushed for too long, then mats may develop in the curly haired type. These can be painful to have brushed out, and if the owner is too aggressive, it can cause injury. Once the mats are beyond your control, it's best to leave it up to a professional groomer who has the tools and skills needed to fix your dog's coat.

Photo Courtesy of Diane Caldemeyer-Reid
www.vonfarawayfarms.com

❝ *No Bernedoodle breeder can say with 100% certainty that their puppies will be completely non-shedding. A new owner should expect their new Bernedoodle to shed some. And if it doesn't, you are one of the lucky ones. "*

Megan Glass
www.glasshousepuppies.com

Bernedoodles don't need to be bathed frequently because washing strips the fur of its natural oils. These oils keep the coat smooth and bright. Unless your dog rolls around in a mud puddle, a clean Bernedoodle only needs to be bathed once every few months.

Bath time can be stressful for a dog that isn't used to it, or if it's had a bad past experience. If your dog tries to do whatever it can to get out of having to take a bath, stay relaxed and try not to get frustrated. Give your dog rewards for each step of the bathing process and give it the opportunity to play once bath time is over.

Before you plop your Bernedoodle in the bathtub, prepare your dog for its bath. If your dog's fur is tangled when you put it in the tub, it probably will still be tangled after shampooing. When fur gets wet, it becomes stretchy, and rough brushing will cause breakage. Let your Bernedoodle feel the water before it's showered with it. Water that's too hot or too cold is uncomfortable and may lead to an aversion to bath time. It's best to ease into the process if it isn't used to being bathed.

Bathe your dog in a tub that has a removable shower head, if possible. You want to have full control of the nozzle. If that isn't available to you, use a cup to pour the water on your dog. Once your dog is used to the water, it's time to shampoo it. Choose a gentle shampoo that's meant for sensitive skin. Your dog probably doesn't need any harsh shampoos for a routine cleaning. A shampoo free of perfumes and dyes works well for most dogs. There are also dog conditioners on the market, but aren't necessary for most dogs, unless the coat is especially tangled or dry. Good nutrition and coat maintenance should eliminate the need for any extra products.

Once your dog is all lathered up, it's time to rinse. It's important to get all of the shampoo off—shampoo residue will make your dog's coat dull and might make it feel itchy. If you shampooed your dog's head, carefully its their head and gently pour water from front to back. Pouring water directly in the face will make your Bernedoodle unhappy. The shampoo can run into the eyes, causing pain and irritation. For this reason, you may just want to avoid shampooing the head and face altogether. Instead, wipe away dirt with a wet washcloth.

To rinse the rest of the body, start at the back and work down to the legs and feet. Rinse until you are positive that there is no more shampoo on the fur or skin.

Finally, it's time to dry your Bernedoodle. Once your dog is out of the bath, gently towel dry its fur. Drying with a hair dryer isn't necessary unless you need your dog dry in a hurry. Some dogs like it, but others might not like the noise and heat. Dry your dog to the point where it won't drip water in your house and let it air dry. Once your dog is dry, give it one final brushing. Dry hair is less prone to breakage than wet hair. Reward your dog for behaving during bath time.

When bathing, be careful not to get water into the eyes and ears. This can be avoided by only washing the face with a washcloth. Otherwise, you may want to gently place a cotton ball into each ear so water cannot become trapped in the ear canal.

Trimming the Nails

Many dogs don't particularly like having their nails trimmed. Even if it doesn't hurt, your Bernedoodle still might find the experience uncomfortable. For that reason, you should have your dog's nails trimmed regularly and reward it for being still while trimming.

Before you even start trimming the nails, get your dog used to having its paw in your hand for a few moments while staying put. Touch the nails and touch different parts of the paw. If it can allow you to do so without squirming or yanking its paw away, give it a treat.

Once it's used to having its paws touched, it's time to get out the clippers. Purchase a pair of nail clippers that are made for large dogs. These should be comfortable and easy to use, even on your big dog's strong nails.

While holding the paw with one hand, carefully trim the end of the nail. This should reduce the sharp point to a flatter point. The nails should be trimmed so that they do not touch the ground while your dog is standing on a flat surface. However, be careful not to cut them too short, or else it will be painful and the nails will bleed. If bleeding occurs, stop it by dipping the nail in a clotting powder or cornstarch. Taking your dog for walks on concrete sidewalks will also help file down its nails.

Frequent trimming is good for preventing problems with the nail. If you let the nails grow too long, the live part of the nail grows further down the end. This makes it harder to trim them without causing bleeding. Also, long nails can put pressure on your dog's feet, which can be very uncomfortable.

If your dog doesn't enjoy having its nails trimmed, start slowly. Trim the back nails and then give it a break. Once you finish cutting the nails, give the dog a treat and praise it. The next time, it will sit still for you if it knows that treats are involved.

Trimming your dog's nails can be a little nerve wracking, so you may opt to have a professional take care of it. Both groomers and veterinarians are experts and know how to trim nails without hurting your dog. If you choose to go with this method, you'll still want to work with your dog to teach it how to sit still and have its paws touched. This will make the whole experience much more pleasant for everyone.

Brushing the Teeth

Good oral hygiene is necessary for the overall health of your Bernedoodle. The bacteria and toxins from advanced gum disease can travel through the dog's blood and damage the organs. Gum disease affects more than just the mouth—many don't realize that it can lead to kidney, heart, and brain disease. Tooth and gum disease can be extremely painful for your dog and can cause difficulties in chewing, not to mention that the smell can be quite unappealing when your dog wants to be near you.

Prevention is key when it comes to fighting off tooth decay and gum disease. Your vet can perform professional teeth cleanings, but they are rather expensive and usually require your dog to be under anesthesia. If you brush your dog's teeth, starting when it's a puppy, you might avoid the need for professional cleanings.

Human toothbrushes and toothpaste probably won't cut it for your pup. Our toothbrushes are too big to fit in dog mouths and our toothpaste cannot be ingested. Luckily, there are lots of different dog toothbrushes and toothpastes out there that are designed with your dog in mind. Some dog toothbrushes are designed to slip over your finger for better control, and others look like a traditional toothbrush, but shaped to fit your dog's mouth. One alternative is to use a child's brush. Make sure the bristles are soft, because your dog's gums can be sensitive and bleed if scrubbed too hard.

Dog toothpastes come in different flavors to encourage your dog to sit still for a brushing. Flavors like chicken, liver, or cheese are tastier to a dog than mint. Surprisingly, these meat flavored pastes will help make your dog's breath smell fresher. These special toothpastes don't create a lather, can be swallowed, and contain enzymes that fight plaque and bacteria.

Photo Courtesy of Alicia Marshall
"Highfalutin Furry Babies Bernedoodles"

Just like with trimming nails, your dog should feel comfortable with having its mouth touched before you start brushing. Carefully lift its lips to reveal the teeth and touch them. You may even try touching them with the brush, without actually scrubbing. Let the dog taste the toothpaste, too. It will feel like it's getting a special treat.

Once your dog is comfortable, you can begin brushing its teeth regularly. Brush gently. Scrubbing too hard can hurt the gums and cause bleeding. Move the brush in a circular motion, brushing each individual tooth for a few seconds before moving on to the next one. Hold the toothbrush at an angle so you can reach the gum line, too. The inside surface may be hard to reach, so don't worry if you can't get to it—the sides of the dog's tongue are rough enough to clean that part.

Once you're finished, reward your dog with lots of praise. However, if it feels safe during the brushing experience, it may feel like it's already being rewarded with the yummy toothpaste.

Cleaning Ears and Eyes

Because Bernedoodles have floppy ears, they are prone to ear infections if moisture gets trapped in the ear canal and has nowhere to go. Your dog's ears are warm places for bacteria to grow, which can lead to a lot of pain and discomfort for your dog. For this reason, an occasional ear cleaning should be done. Depending on the cleanliness of your dog's ears, you can clean them when you bathe your dog.

To clean your dog's ears, you can use water, or better yet, a solution made specifically for cleaning the gunk out of ears. Dog ear cleaning solutions can be purchased at your vet's office. Squirt the cleaning liquid into your dog's ear and use the outside of your dog's ear to rub the liquid into the ear canal. After a quick massage, take a cotton ball and carefully wipe away any discharge from the outer part of the ear. Do not dig into the ear canal, because this can cause serious damage to the delicate inner ear. If you're concerned about damaging your dog's ears, you can ask your vet for a lesson during your next check-up.

Sometimes, small amounts of dirt or tear residue build up under your dog's eyes. To clean them, take a damp rag or cotton ball and gently wipe under the eye. Never touch your dog's eyes or use soaps to clean them. When

Photo Courtesy of Diane Caldemeyer-Reid
www.vonfarawayfarms.com

bathing your dog, try to avoid shampooing the face altogether. The eyes are sensitive and are easily irritated by chemicals.

Professional Grooming

" *It is important to know that you will need to do some grooming with the Bernedoodle. It is not the rigorous grooming required for the Standard Poodle but there is grooming involved."*

Diane Caldemeyer-Reid
www.vonfarawayfarms.com

Because the Bernedoodle is a Poodle Crossbreed, it will need the occasional trim at the groomer's to keep it looking pretty and to prevent fur matting. The curlier your dog is, the more it needs to be groomed. Every six to eight weeks or so, bring your dog to your groomer for a little trim.

If there's a particular way you want your Bernedoodle to be groomed, you should find a picture to show your groomer. Discuss the trim before it happens so you won't be shocked or upset by what your groomer has done.

Your dog's groomer will trim the hair around the eyes and ears, as well as trim around the face and cut out any matted fur. Not only will this make your dog look nice, it will also help it see better and keep hair out of sensitive areas. Unless you specify a specific type of cut, your Bernedoodle will have a natural-looking cut.

A good grooming routine can keep your Bernedoodle healthy and happy. It only takes a few minutes a day to ensure that your dog's coat is soft, its teeth are clean, and its nails are at a comfortable length. By keeping up with home grooming, you can save yourself a lot of money by preventing problems before they escalate to the point where a professional is needed. There are some tasks, like trimming hair around delicate areas, that are best left to the professionals. But, just like a healthy diet, good hygiene can improve the life of your Bernedoodle.

CHAPTER 13

" *Parents are tested and healthy but that is not always a guarantee. It is always good to take your pup to your own vet for a full health checkup the first week. It will give your vet a baseline and you peace of mind."*

Diane Caldemeyer-Reid
www.vonfarawayfarms.com

BASIC HEALTH CARE

When you become a dog owner, there are few things more important than the health of your furry family member. Because a dog can't tell you its symptoms, it's up to the owner to make sure everything is okay with its body. By knowing what your dog's good health looks like and watching for cues that your dog is not well, you'll be able to know when your dog needs to see a vet.

Regardless of your Bernedoodle's health, regular vet care should be a part of its life from the time it's a puppy to the end of its life. Sometimes costs can add up, but with good preventative care, many procedures and medications can be avoided. Regular checkups allow vets to find potential problems before they get out of hand. Good healthcare will allow your dog to be happy and healthy into advanced age.

Visiting the Vet

Before you even bring your new Bernedoodle home, choose a veterinarian for your dog. This way, you know where to go if something unexpected happens. If you're purchasing a dog from a breeder that does health guarantees, there's a good chance you'll need a vet appointment within the first week of having your pup in your home. This way, both the breeder and the owner are protected from any unseen circumstance in the health of the dog.

If you're taking your dog to the vet for the first time, you may have no idea what is going on. This is a good time to ask your veterinarian about your dog's health. Vets are a great resource to use when it comes to just about anything relating to your pet. They have the expertise and experience to give you credible information about your Bernedoodle.

At each checkup, you can expect to see the same examinations performed on your dog. Your dog will most likely be weighed first. This is a good way to compare the weight of your dog from year to year so you know if your dog is losing or gaining too much weight at any time. The vet will also listen to your dog's heart and lungs and check its temperature. Your vet will use his or her hands to check for any lumps or protrusions from the body, and will also check your dog's skin and coat. Next, he or she will look at the eyes, ears, and mouth. Finally, your vet will administer any vaccinations if necessary.

While this all seems very straightforward and simple, going to the vet can be stressful for a dog. Some dogs get upset by being in a new place or being around new people or animals. Fortunately, as an owner, there are things you can do to put your dog at ease.

If possible, get your dog used to the idea of riding in a car. If car rides are traumatizing to begin with, the resulting vet visit might not make it feel any better. If possible, take your dog to visit the veterinarian's office and meet your vet without having a checkup. Chances are, your dog won't remember your vet from visit to vis-

Photo Courtesy of Steve Hetherington

it, but if it can survive a short visit with no problems, once the real checkup rolls around, it will be a little more prepared. End all visits with treats and affection.

Another issue dogs have with the vet is that there are strange people and animals around. If your dog isn't used to being around strangers, it may feel threatened. This can be dangerous for a vet because a scared dog can become aggressive without much notice. Socialization is key here. Allow your dog to have some positive interactions with friends, family, and other dogs. Soon, it will learn that it can trust others not to hurt it.

Finally, prepare your dog to be touched. You may even want to run through a sort of "mock checkup" with it, just so it gets used to the idea of being checked out. Run your hands along its body, peek into its ears, and pull its lips back and look at the teeth. If your dog knows basic commands at this point, practice "sit" and "lie down" before you go. This will make checkups easier on everyone involved. Regular checkups are very important for your Bernedoodle, so you don't want any reason not to go.

Preventative Care

Whether your dog has caught a virus at the dog park or swallowed a sock, some visits to the vet cannot be avoided. However, many injuries and illnesses can be prevented. You may find that these preventative measures may cost more than doing nothing and hoping for the best, but a vet bill for treating preventable illnesses will exceed that cost. Think of preventative care as investing in your dog's health. Besides, you'll want to make sure your dog lives a long, healthy life.

In this section, we will examine different types of common health issues in dogs and ways to treat them on your own. Of course, if you find that your dog's healthcare goes beyond your expertise, it's best to get advice straight from your veterinarian. Even well-meaning owners make mistakes from time to time, but remember that your veterinarian knows more than a stranger's blog on dog health can teach you.

External Parasites

If your dog ever goes outside (which it absolutely should) it is at risk for picking up some sort of parasite. Fleas and ticks are two external parasites that can cause problems if they aren't treated immediately.

Fleas are tiny insects that latch on to your dog's skin and suck its blood. This causes a reaction in animals that makes them incredibly itchy. Excessive scratching can lead to open sores that can become infected. Overall, these pests will make your dog very uncomfortable.

The tricky thing about fleas is that they reproduce quickly. A few fleas can turn into a hundred in a matter of days. When your dog comes inside, they can spread to other pets or people. Because they are so small, you might not be able to notice them until they have already laid their eggs.

Ticks, on the other hand, are easier to notice, but only if you're looking in the right place. When you pet your dog, especially after a long walk in the woods, you may notice a small bump on its skin. These creatures start out small, but expand to become quite large when fully engorged with blood. Once you find them, they need to be removed. While this can be an icky task, it's relatively simple.

When you remove a tick, grasp it towards the mouth and pull up. They may be hard to separate from the skin, but it's better to remove them in their entirety than to leave bits behind. Once you remove it, make sure to destroy it so it doesn't find its way back to your dog for another meal.

One reason why these external parasites are so dangerous is because they can transmit diseases that can cause serious illness. Also, when your dog loses a lot of blood to these critters, it can cause anemia.

There are a few ways to kill these parasites once your dog is infected. You can purchase special shampoos, collars, skin treatments, and even oral medications that can kill the parasites and their eggs. Keep in mind that these use certain chemicals that can be harmful in incorrect doses. Check with a vet before using these products and follow the directions on the package.

Photo Courtesy of Alex Byrnes

Internal Parasites

Internal parasites, like worms, can be harder to spot because they live inside the animal. Roundworms and tapeworms are large enough to be spotted in your dog's stool, but hookworms and whipworms are harder to see. These parasites can cause weight loss, intestinal blockage, vomiting, or bloody diarrhea. Just like with external parasites, if these consume enough of your dog's blood, it can become severely anemic.

If you suspect your dog has intestinal worms, you will need to give your vet a stool sample to confirm that it has worms, and to figure out what kind they are. Next, your vet will give you a medication for your pup to get rid of the worms. Eventually, they will be cleared from the body. When this happens, make sure your dog does not re-infect itself. Clean all fecal matter from your yard, especially if your dog tends to eat its excrement. If your dog goes to the dog park, keep an eye on where it goes and what it's doing. After handling your dog's feces, wash your hands thoroughly—a dog's intestinal worms can spread to the owner.

Heartworm is another parasite that is deadly to dogs. It enters the body through a bite from an infected mosquito. Once a dog becomes infected, the worms will travel to the lungs, heart, and blood vessels, making it difficult for your dog to take part in every day activities. Left untreated, heartworms are fatal to dogs.

Fortunately, heartworm can be prevented. Heartworm medications can be administered monthly, which will keep your dog safe from these parasites. If an unprotected dog gets heartworm and it is caught early enough, it can be treated. However, it is an expensive process that includes x-rays, blood tests, and injections.

Supplements and Holistic Treatments

Many humans take vitamin supplements to give them a boost where their own diet is lacking. Sometimes, supplements are necessary when people have a diagnosed deficiency in some area of their nutrition. While not all vitamin users have a medical reason to take them, it makes consumers feel like they are making a healthy choice. It's no wonder many pet owners give their dogs supplements as well.

If your dog is eating a quality dog food, there probably isn't a need for extra supplements. Dog foods already come with necessary vitamins and minerals. Giving a dog a multivitamin on top of its food may be overdoing it. Some minerals, like calcium, can cause growth problems in large dogs if they ingest too much. Unless your dog is deficient, or is eating a homemade food that lacks essential nutrients, a vitamin supplement may just be a waste of money.

Of course, there are some nutrients that may help your dog if its body shows signs that it needs it. Check with a vet before adding anything to your dog's diet. While you may believe that your dog's dull coat is a result of not getting enough fat,

Photo Courtesy of Megan Glass
www.glasshousepuppies.com

a vet may test for hormone imbalances or other conditions that would require different treatments.

For large dogs, glucosamine and chondroitin are commonly used to prevent and improve joint damage. Fish oil can give your dog a healthy shine to its coat and improve various body functions. Antioxidants, like the kinds found in fruits and vegetables, also play different roles in the body and may even slow down signs of aging.

When administering supplements to your dog, always stick to the suggested dose. Just because a little dose might cause some improvement doesn't mean that a larger dose will have the same effect on a larger scale. Also, keep in mind that the supplements you buy are probably not regulated and may not even contain what the labels say they contain. Find a reputable seller for these types of products.

When a dog is sick, some owners prefer to use holistic treatments rather than pharmaceuticals because they believe that plant sources provide a more natural remedy. While herbs and other types of supplements may have a medicinal effect on your dog, it's not always best. Sometimes, these types of treatments can cause harmful side effects or are not as effective as drugs. If you prefer to go the holistic route, speak with your vet to see if it's a good idea. Some therapies are worth a try, and others aren't, but your vet will be able to tell you what's best.

Vaccinations

If you own a dog, it needs to be vaccinated for its own safety and the safety of others. Not only do vaccinations keep your Bernedoodle safe, they lessen the spread of dangerous diseases. Your vet will be able to tell you which vaccinations your dog needs and when they need to be given.

There's a good chance your dog will already have had some vaccinations before you even take it home. Good animal shelters will make sure their dogs are up to date on their important shots before letting them go home with you. Parvovirus, rabies, distemper, and hepatitis vaccines are necessary for your dog's health. Other vaccinations like the ones for bordetella, lyme disease, and various respiratory diseases may be recommended by your vet.

While some vaccinations are administered as early as five weeks, some are not given until after the twelfth week. In many cases, puppies are purchased and taken to a new home before they receive all of their shots. This makes them vulnerable in situations where they may interact with unvaccinated dogs. However, this is during the prime time to have them socialize with other dogs. If possible, keep your dog's interactions with other dogs limited to ones that are vaccinated. Find a friend with a vaccinated pup for a play date, or take your Bernedoodle to a training course that requires vaccinations in adult dogs.

Once your puppy has received all of its shots, it will require booster shots every few years or so. Your veterinarian will keep everything on record, so you won't have to worry about remembering when your dog needs its shots. There are even laws about certain vaccinations, like rabies, so your vet will know what's required by your state.

Pet Insurance

Because vet bills can add up quickly, some owners choose to buy pet insurance, just in case of an unforeseen circumstance. Few people prepare for serious injury or illness happening to their dogs, but it's important to be prepared for it. Often times, owners choose to euthanize their beloved family members because they cannot afford their treatment. Pet insurance may make it easier to give your dog the care it needs.

You'll want to do some research to find the best policy for your Bernedoodle. Figure out if you need a policy that covers preexisting conditions or genetic diseases. Find one that covers many different treatments and medications that your dog may need within its lifetime.

Even if you decide you'd rather not buy an insurance policy for your dog, it's a good idea to set aside money for it in case of an emergency. Set aside at least a few hundred dollars for emergencies separate from your regular checkup budget, so an emergency visit to the vet won't cause too much financial strain.

A Bernedoodle that feels good is a joy to be around. While we may not always connect behavior with health, if a dog suddenly starts acting up or isn't as playful as usual, it can be a sign of poor health. Proper care will also extend the lifespan and give a higher quality of life. Whenever possible, take preventative measures when it comes to healthcare. It's cheaper and easier to prevent an illness or injury than it is to treat it.

Photo Courtesy of Alicia Marshall
"Highfalutin Furry Babies Bernedoodles"

CHAPTER 14

ADVANCED BERNEDOODLE HEALTH

❝ *The Bernedoodle breed is fairly new, and a complete picture of the health concerns of the Bernedoodle is still emerging. Thankfully, Bernedoodles do seem to have a hybrid vigor, although there are no guarantees. Incidences of cancer, a major concern of the Bernese Mountain Dog, seem not to be as common of an issue with the Bernedoodle. However, Bernedoodles are prone to some conditions such as hip and elbow dysplasia, and skin and eye conditions. "*

Brian Montgomery
www.bmdfamilyfarms.com

Some health conditions are tough to prevent. Just like humans, dogs can be predisposed to certain genetic diseases. These genetic conditions vary from breed to breed. Typically, large dogs will have similar conditions to other large dogs, due to how their skeletal system forms as puppies.

Bernedoodles are prone to inherit certain conditions, but it doesn't necessarily mean that your dog will develop any diseases. Even if it does, many won't appear until the dog is in the later years of its life. However, if you know what to look out for, there's a better chance you'll know when to take your dog to the vet.

Breeding plays a role in whether or not a Bernedoodle will develop a disease. Good breeders will only use dogs that have passed health screenings and have not shown signs of illness. Also, they know which particular genetic traits can be crossed with other particular genetic traits. In some breeds, crossing dogs with certain traits will produce a very unique-looking dog, but one that will suffer from a wide range of health problems. Similarly, if an unskilled breeder attempts to breed a dog much smaller than it should be, often times it results in an unhealthy dog. Good breeders know how to minimize risk in their puppies.

But because all dogs are different, it's best to know what to look for. This section will cover common health conditions found in Bernedoodles. Also, because crossbreeds like Bernedoodles show traits from the Poodle and Bernese Mountain Dog lineage, this section will also discuss common conditions in those breeds.

Common Ailments in Bernedoodles

Because the Bernedoodle is a crossbreed, it is likely to have fewer genetic conditions than a purebred dog. This is because there is a deeper gene pool, due to the wider selection of dogs to breed from. This results in less inbreeding which can occasionally produce some strange results.

When genetic illnesses are connected to recessive genes, that means the effects will only show up if both the Poodle and the Bernese Mountain Dog share the same genetic conditions. However, some Bernedoodles have different proportions of Poodle and Bernese Mountain Dog in them, so it all depends on who the parents are.

Because this crossbreed hasn't been around for very long and isn't widely recognized by breeders, it's hard to say what illnesses can be attributed to the breed. With time, breeders will begin to see common patterns in the Bernedoodle's heath, like they would with pure breeds.

Bernedoodles, like all large dogs, are more likely to have hip and elbow dysplasia than smaller dogs. Hip dysplasia is a condition that occurs when the leg bone doesn't properly fit into the hip joint. Similarly, elbow dysplasia is the improper fit of the elbow joint. Often times, this occurs when puppies grow too quickly, usually due to nutrition imbalances.

When the bones and joints don't fit how they should, it can cause a lot of pain when your dog walks and jumps. In serious cases, it can lead to complete lameness in the affected limbs. As your Bernedoodle ages, you may be more likely to see symptoms of arthritis in dogs with joint dysplasia.

If your dog suddenly has trouble doing activities it would normally do, or acts anxious when you touch near its joints, it may have a joint disorder that needs special attention.

Photo Courtesy of Nathan Salomon

Bernedoodles are also susceptible to different kinds of eye diseases. Progressive Retinal Atrophy is a group of eye diseases that cause gradual blindness in dogs. With this condition, the retina slowly deteriorates until all vision is lost. This typically starts out as night blindness, but can worsen over time. Many times, the dog does not become fully blind until it is in their later stages of life. While this can be an inconvenience for an old dog, it will learn to adapt to its limited vision. In fact, owners might not know the severity of their dog's sight impairment because it maneuvers around the home so well.

Many dogs are also susceptible to different types of allergies. Bernedoodles are good for people with allergies, but they can suffer from allergies themselves. Dogs can be allergic to certain foods, chemicals, or environmental factors. It's possible for your dog to be allergic to more than one thing.

Food allergies can be easy to avoid, but it can take a while to figure out which ingredient causes the reaction. There may be some trial and error with finding the right food, but once you figure it out, your dog should feel much better. Some pet owners believe that grains like corn, wheat, and soy cause allergic reactions, while others have issues with artificial flavors, colors, and preservatives.

Environmental and chemical allergies can also leave your dog feeling itchy and miserable. Certain plants or shampoos cause this type of allergic response. The dog may scratch at its skin more and create open wounds. Because avoiding the outdoors isn't going to work for an active Bernedoodle, veterinarians can recommend products that help relieve the itching. If you notice your dog is itchy after a bath, try a shampoo that's made for sensitive skin and rinse well.

Common Ailments in Bernese Mountain Dogs

Other than a few common conditions found in large dogs, it's difficult to make a direct link from the Bernedoodle crossbreed to any specific illness. That's why it's also important to know what conditions are common with the parents. Bernese Mountain Dogs have their own list of common health concerns. Unfortunately, this breed has a longer list than most breeds. But when crossed with a Poodle, their health concerns decrease and their life expectancy increases.

Because Bernese Mountain Dogs have a deep chest, it makes them susceptible to gastric torsion, or bloat. This occurs when a dog eats too much at once, or eats too quickly. The stomach fills with gas that cannot be expelled so the stomach twists. Not only does it cause gastric distress, it cuts off the blood flow to other parts of the body. When this occurs, the dog will dry heave, salivate more than usual, and may even go into shock. If it isn't dealt with promptly, it may cause death. Fortunately, this can be prevented by controlling how much and how quickly a Berner eats its meals and if it exercises strenuously after eating.

Photo Courtesy of Cheryl Ziegler

This breed also commonly suffers from conditions that affect blood and blood flow. Von Willebrand's Disease is a condition that makes it hard for your dog's blood to clot. That means that a small injury or surgical procedure can cause excessive bleeding, internally and externally. This condition is usually apparent within the first five years of a dog's life and can be treated with medication; complications can be avoided with special precautions. Berners also occasionally suffer from a blood vessel defect that causes blood to bypass the liver, making it hard for the blood to be cleaned of toxins. This also shows up early in life and can cause serious health complications without surgical intervention. Symptoms include hypoglycemia, lack of hunger, stunted growth, and urinary tract abnormalities.

Different types of cancers are especially common in Bernese Mountain Dogs, partially accounting for their short average lifespan. Depending on the type of cancer, symptoms can vary. If you notice any abnormal lump, bleeding, or difficulties with exercise or daily activity, talk to your vet. The sooner the vet diagnoses the cancer, the more effective treatments will be. Some cancerous tumors can be removed through surgery, but others will require medication.

With an average lifespan almost double the Bernese Mountain Dog's, the Poodle has a different list of potential health concerns. Epilepsy is a common condition in Poodles. Seizures may not always present themselves in the manner you might think. In addition to shaking, a dog might run erratically, hide, or stumble around. While this is scary for an owner to witness, with the right treatment, the seizures can improve.

Sebaceous Adenitis is a very common condition in Standard Poodles. A dog's skin has glands that produce sebum, or an oily substance that keeps the skin moisturized and protected. With this condition, the glands become inflamed and cease to produce oil. This results in dry, infected skin. This can be confused for other conditions because dry or itchy skin is a common symptom for a lot of disorders.

Poodles are also known for having different types of hormone disorders. Some increase the production of cortisol and others affect the adrenal gland. Depending on if the dog produces too many hormones or not enough, you may see lethargy, vomiting, excessive urination, and poor appetite. These conditions can be controlled with medication.

Finally, some Poodles suffer from hypothyroidism. This occurs when the thyroid doesn't function as well as it should. Symptoms include lethargy, dry skin, epilepsy, and weight gain. This can be treated with medication or possibly improved with a dietary change. It is believed that iodine can improve thyroid function in dogs. Iodine is found in seaweed, which is often added to dog foods in supplemental amounts.

While all of these medical conditions sound frightening, remember that not all dogs will experience all (or any) of them. These are just a few conditions that breeders have noticed recurring in the breed. With proper breeding, a dog can go its whole life without one of these diseases popping up. Also, crossbreeds tend to have fewer of these conditions because breeders aren't breeding dogs with the same medical tendencies together. It may seem like a lot to worry about, but as long as you can spot unusual symptoms in your dog and go to a vet with your concerns, your Bernedoodle will be in good hands.

Illness and Injury Prevention

❝ *Genetic testing of breeding stock can reduce the risks of passing down congenital conditions of both the Poodle and the Bernese Mountain Dog. A reputable breeder will be performing these tests to ensure the genetic health of both parents before any breeding occurs. "*

Brian Montgomery
www.bmdfamilyfarms.com

When it comes to your dog's health, prevention is everything. It's much easier to maintain your Bernedoodle's good health than it is to fix problems. When left to its own devices, a dog can get itself into all sorts of trouble. Whether it's taking part in dangerous activities or eating strange things, your little adventurer is unwittingly putting itself at risk. Don't panic—if you can catch your dog doing something it shouldn't be and correct it, you'll be able to give it a little more freedom as it grows up.

When it comes to injuries, it's hard to prevent some accidents. Because your Bernedoodle may have delicate joints, try to keep it from jumping off of tall objects. When a dog's joints already don't fit together well, a lot of pressure on them can cause pain and inflammation. Don't let the fear of injury keep you from letting your dog play, but if it likes to hop up on your furniture, only to hop right down, you might want to teach it that it's best to stay off in the first place.

Photo Courtesy of Alicia Marshall "Highfalutin Furry Babies Bernedoodles"

Another way to keep your dog's joints healthy is to keep it at a healthy weight. An overweight dog puts extra stress on its bones and joints, which might cause the cartilage to wear out faster. Unless your dog has an untreated medical condition, its weight is a result of its caloric intake and exercise (or lack thereof). The dog owner is responsible for giving the right amount of food to replace the calories burned during the day. Overfeeding or a lack of exercise can cause weight gain that can result in injury. Good, healthy foods and at least one good walk a day can help your dog maintain a healthy weight.

Many medical concerns can be prevented, or at least improved, with a good diet. A dog's diet is much more than just a source of calories. Dogs need the right proportions of carbs, protein, and fats, plus the right mix of vitamins and minerals. Nutrient deficiencies can harm organ function and shorten their lifespan.

For instance, foods with antioxidants fight free radicals that cause damage to the body and may even accelerate cancer growth. A diet with carrots, berries, and leafy greens may protect your dog's body from toxins that cause disease. If your dog food doesn't contain these types of produce, you can even use them for training treats. Foods with glucosamine, found in chicken cartilage, are good for your dog's joints. There are many good nutrients found in quality dog foods that can help your dog stay healthy and fight off disease.

There's no telling what conditions your Bernedoodle may have later in life, but with good care, it should be able to live a long, healthy life. Because a dog can't tell you when it's not feeling well, it's up to the owner to notice symptoms and get the medical attention it needs. Genetic conditions can appear without warning, but if your Bernedoodle is already in excellent shape, it will be more likely to bounce back from whatever comes its way.

CHAPTER 15

TRAVELLING WITH BERNEDOODLES

" *I have owned more breeds of dogs than I can count. And I have never seen a breed that desires to be loved more than the Bernedoodle."*

Megan Glass
www.glasshousepuppies.com

Photo Courtesy of Maggie Box
www.angelviewdoodles.com

Once your Bernedoodle enters your family, you'll want to start treating it like a real member of the family. This means that wherever you go, your dog comes too.

Transporting a dog can be tricky sometimes. It needs to be properly restrained in a moving vehicle for both the driver's safety and its own. Also, going to a new place can be terrifying for dogs. If they aren't used to going on road trips, it can be quite traumatizing. Eventually, a scared dog can develop anxiety that makes it nearly impossible to take it anywhere.

But with a little preparation and some trial runs, your dog will love cruising around with you in no time.

Dog Carriers and Restraints

It is imperative to restrain your Bernedoodle in one way or another when it travels with you. A wandering dog can be a huge distraction in your vehicle. Plus, if unrestrained, it will become a projectile in the event of an accident.

There are different kinds of safety restraints and dog carriers on the market to suit your needs. A crate is a good multipurpose tool to have in your home because it can double as a safety restraint and a safe place for your dog to stay while home alone. As an added bonus, your carsick Bernedoodle won't be able to see out the window, which may help with motion sickness.

If you don't want a bulky crate in your car, you may opt for a safety harness. These harnesses are worn by your dog and then clipped into your car's seatbelts.

Photo Courtesy of Maggie Box
www.angelviewdoodles.com

Just as you would do with a child, place your dog in the backseat of your car. In the event of an accident, this is the safest place. These restraints work best when tightly secured to your car.

For large dogs, like the Bernedoodle, you may choose a barrier method. These only work in SUV or minivan-type vehicles that have a flat space in the back. A mesh barrier can block access to the rest of the car by covering the space above the back row of seats. If you're on a long trip with a restless dog, this allows it to stretch its legs a little more. Unfortunately, because there is plenty of space to move around, it is more likely to be injured in an accident.

No matter which safety method you use, make sure your Bernedoodle never rides in a car without some sort of restraint. Also, make sure the restraint is appropriate for its size. As your Bernedoodle grows, so should the safety restraint.

Crate Training

A crate is perhaps the easiest way to transport a dog from one place to another. Not only does it keep your dog safe, but it also gives it a sense of security. Crate training can make traveling much easier, plus it's helpful in the home, too.

Your Bernedoodle's crate should always be a nice, comfortable place to be. It should not be used as a "time out" place for punishment because then your dog will be hesitant to go into the crate because it will associate it with negative emotions. It will take some time to get your dog fully crate trained, so be patient and positive.

First, let your pup check out the new crate in a safe environment. Put the crate in a common area where you and your family spend time and let it look around at its leisure. Make the crate more comfortable by placing a blanket or a dog bed on the inside. After a while, it might want to go inside a have a peek for itself—it will want to know what this exciting box is all about. If your dog has no interest, toss a toy or a treat in the crate. If it really isn't taking the bait, put a trail of treats all the way up to the crate. If it doesn't want to go in, try again later. Forcing it into the crate will only make your dog want to avoid it altogether.

Once you get to the point where your dog is comfortable with the concept of going in the crate, start feeding it in the crate. You may want to temporarily put the food bowls on the inside and let it enter to eat its meals. This will make crate time a positive experience because it's rewarded with food for hanging out in the crate for as long as it takes to eat a meal. Once it's comfortable, try shutting the door for a while.

Now that the dog is comfortable with the crate, keep it in there for longer periods of time. Give a command like "crate" and reward it when it goes in the crate on command. Start doing this when you leave the house for short periods of time.

Photo Courtesy of Jean Etzel

Slowly extend the amount of time you are away, and eventually you can leave it in there for a couple hours at a time.

Keep in mind that you may hear whining when just starting out with your puppy. When your dog is whining, it may be telling you that it needs to use the bathroom, especially at night. However, it may be making noise because it's bored and wants attention from you, or feeling anxious about being alone. If you have good reason to think your dog is whining for the potty, let it out. Otherwise, ignore the whines. If you let it out every time it whines, it learns that when it whines, it will be rewarded by being let out to play. Only open the crate if the dog is quiet. When starting out, stay within its line of sight. Many times, new puppies just need to know that they haven't been abandoned. Give this process a few weeks of gradual practice while keeping it positive.

Once your dog is comfortable being in the crate at home, then you can take it on the road. A crate is sturdy and can easily be restrained in the car, so you won't have to worry about it flying around. Plus, a nervous dog can feel safe in its crate if it already uses it for sanctuary.

Car Rides

Some dogs love feeling the wind through their fur, but for others, car trips are frightening. It can take some time to get used to riding in a moving vehicle, so as with any form of training, start slow and keep things positive. When you bring your dog home for the first time, you can get a feel for how it behaved. Did it sit still, or was it panting and crying?

Photo Courtesy of Jean Etzel

If your Bernedoodle loves car rides, you're in luck! Just pop it in the crate and take it everywhere you go. Because it's possible for dogs to get carsick too, try to avoid feeding right before a trip. You'll also want to make sure it uses the bathroom so you don't have to worry about cleaning up messes.

If not, there are some things you can do to make it feel a little more at ease. First, let your dog spend some time in your parked vehicle. Give treats or favorite toys to play with. If it's okay with that, start driving around the block. Over time, gradually increase the amount of time you drive. When you get back home, give your dog lots of praise and reward it with play time. Keep practicing driving around with your dog until it feel less anxious about riding in your vehicle.

Sometimes, no matter what you do, some dogs just tend to get carsick. If restricting food before a trip and keeping your dog away from the window don't work, you can ask your veterinarian about medication to help with your dog's nausea. If your dog feels sick when it's in a car, it might develop an aversion to cars.

Once all of these concerns are addressed, it's time to hit the road! On long car trips, don't forget to bring all of your dog's essential items. This includes plenty of water, food (if you'll be away from home during the next meal), toys, waste bags, and a leash and collar with identification. When you stop to let your dog use the bathroom and stretch its legs, it needs to be on a leash. A new place can be overwhelming and you don't want your pup to run off.

Flying

Flying can be stressful for humans, so owners can expect it to be tough on their pet, too. There are so many strange sounds and smells, plus your dog might not be with you as you fly. For this reason, try to avoid flying with your dog when you can reasonably drive.

However, sometimes, it's not possible to drive to your destination and you need to bring your Bernedoodle with you. Unless your Bernedoodle is a puppy over the age of ten weeks or registered as a working dog, it will not be able to ride in the cabin with you. This means that it will be put into the cargo hold. Each airline has different rules regarding dogs in the cabin.

It's hard to prepare your dog for a long flight when it's never been in an airplane before. Unfortunately, it's not as simple as going for a short test flight with your pup. The best way to prepare your dog is to crate train it well enough that it won't panic if left alone for too long.

If you are taking an international flight with your dog, you will need to provide food and water for your dog, plus a favorite toy or blanket to comfort it. Make sure your dog is wearing some sort of identification and write your name and contact information on the crate as well. The last place you want your dog to get lost is somewhere between one country and another.

Whenever possible, fly direct flights. It can be a lot more expensive for you, but the fewer stops you make, the fewer mistakes can be made when handling your dog.

Keep in mind that different airlines have different policies regarding transporting dogs. Also, depending on where you're going, you may need to have vet records to prove your dog is in good health and has all of its shots. When you begin planning your trip, contact your airline to get all the information you need to feel at ease with bringing your Bernedoodle along.

Hotel Stays

Once your arrive at your destination, you'll probably be staying in an unfamiliar place. First, you'll want to ensure that your accommodations allow dogs in the first place. Some will charge heavy fines if you're caught with an animal in their rooms. Most hotels that allow pets will have an added charge per pet.

If possible, book a hotel with dog-friendly surroundings. A hotel near a park may be more ideal than one in the middle of a busy city for your dog. If it's used to doing its business on grass and can only walk on concrete, it may be confused about what to do. Also, try to get a room on the ground floor. It will be much easier to get outside when necessary, and you can avoid taking the elevator or stairs.

If you transported your dog to the hotel in a crate, then its bed is already sorted. If not, you should bring its bed or a familiar blanket to cuddle up on. If you plan on leaving your dog alone during the day, make sure you give it plenty of exercise first. A bored dog may become destructive and noisy. Try to keep your Bernedoodle nearby whenever possible, because it might not like being alone in a strange place.

Kenneling and Dog Sitters

Sometimes, it's just too difficult to take your Bernedoodle with you. When considering taking your dog along on your travels, think about how much time it will have to stay alone, plus the degree of stress traveling with place on it. When it isn't worth the amount of stress it'll be under, you can find an alternative for care.

Think of a kennel as a hotel for dogs. There, your dog will have its own space with employees to take care of its every need. It will always have someone to take it to the bathroom, to give it exercise, and to feed it. It will be in a secure area, so you

Photo Courtesy of Alicia Marshall
"Highfalutin Furry Babies Bernedoodles"

won't have to worry about it escaping and getting lost. Because it's in a place built for dogs, you won't have to worry about it destroying your belongings.

Talk to people in your community to find a good kennel. When you've narrowed down your search, visit one to check out their facilities. You want to make sure everything is clean, the dogs are allowed to have separate spaces, and all animals are up to date on their shots. Talk to some employees and watch them in action. Do they seem knowledgeable and friendly towards the other dogs? If so, book a space for your dog long before your trip. You don't want to find yourself out of options because the kennels are all booked up.

For some dogs, a kennel may not be a good option. If your dog has not been properly socialized to be around other dogs, going from being the only dog at home to a place with a lot of dogs can be stressful. Your town might also be lacking kennel facilities, or they might not be up to your standard. When this occurs, you'll need a dog sitter.

A dog sitter can put your dog at ease by keeping it in a familiar environment. Whether this is just a neighbor stopping over a few times a day to check up on your dog, or a hired professional staying in your home, you'll want someone you can trust with your dog. If you don't have a friend who can take on the commitment, there are people you can hire to stay with your dog. This can be expensive, but it's worth it to know your Bernedoodle is okay while you're absent.

Before your trip, have your dog sitter come over to the home to spend some time with your dog. Have the sitter play with your dog and give it treats. Your dog might not remember the sitter, but it's more likely to be at ease spending time with a stranger if you're there the first time. Hiring a pet sitter allows your dog to have one-on-one time with someone in the comfort of its own home.

Before choosing a kennel or a sitter, think about your dog's socialization skills, the possibility of separation anxiety, and your budget. When leaving town, you'll want to make sure your dog is in good hands and that the person caring for it will contact you with any concerns.

Tips and Tricks for Traveling with a Dog

Before you fasten your dog in the car or deliver it to the airline for a flight, make sure it gets plenty of exercise. Not only will this keep it from getting restless, but may even tire it out enough to get it to take a short nap. A nap will help keep it occupied until it's time to get out and stretch its legs again. When riding in a car, let your dog out of the car every three to four hours to keep it from feeling too cooped up.

Don't forget to pack your dog's favorite toys. Not only will these be comforting, they will also help entertain your dog. Having something to chew on will also keep it from attempting to destroy its crate.

Any time you travel with your dog, make sure it gets a reward when it's all over. Over time, it will learn to associate travel with treats or a long walk and will be more inclined to cooperate with you the next time you call it to the car.

If you have an anxious Bernedoodle that gets nervous no matter what you do, try to bring an extra person along on your travels. One owner cannot be responsible for both driving and comforting the dog. Another person can sit next to your Bernedoodle and reassure it that it isn't alone in the strange moving contraption. An extra hand is especially good when bringing your Bernedoodle home for the first time because everything will be new and puppies frighten easily when they're alone.

Going to a new place can be exciting for a dog. However, it's hard to know how a dog will react to strange surroundings. By keeping as many familiar factors as possible, you'll help your dog stay calm and comfortable. A little preparation goes a long way toward making your dog happy during a potentially stressful time.

CHAPTER 16

LIFE WITH AN AGING BERNEDOODLE

Some owners think that once they get their Bernedoodle through the long puppy stage, their work is over. Raising a new puppy is hard work and it gets easier as they grow up, but dogs need specialized attention at all stages of life.

After a long and happy life, you may notice that your Bernedoodle is starting to slow down. This is a natural part of life. Keep in mind that aging dogs have different needs than young, spry pups.

Photo Courtesy of Megan Glass
www.glasshousepuppies.com

Basics of Senior Dog Care

First, you might want to determine if your dog has reached senior status, or if there's something else going on. As opposed to the Bernese Mountain Dog that becomes a senior around the age of six or so, the Bernedoodle has a lifespan of around twelve to fifteen years. Your dog may show signs of slowing down around eight or nine.

Senior dogs often begin to lose their sense of sight and hearing. You may notice that your well-trained dog doesn't listen to you when you tell it to sit. While it may be a behavior issue, it's likely because it can't hear your command.

When a dog gradually loses sight, it may still be able to navigate in familiar surroundings, but may also be easily startled. This may be because it can't see or hear you approach, despite the fact that you may not notice any sight impairment.

Your aging dog's activity level will change too. Instead of going on short runs, you dog may be more comfortable with walking. A dog that once sprinted circles around the backyard may slow down to a trot when retrieving toys. If your dog appears to be in worse shape, don't push it too hard to return to its previous fitness level. Its organs and skeletal system may not be able to support strenuous activity levels. Injuries are more likely to occur when you push your old dog past its comfort level.

Especially in dogs prone to hip and elbow dysplasia, arthritic joints signal old age. You may notice that your dog is slow to get up from a prone position or stiff first thing in the morning. While you may try giving your dog joint supplements to counter the effects of old age, understand that this is a normal part of an old dog's life. If your dog is stiff after long periods of rest, give it a few moments to slowly warm up its joints before exercise. If it will let you, you may even want to try gently massaging its sore limbs. Even the warmth from your hands can relieve a little pain.

You may also find that your dog's behavior changes as it ages. Your friendly, excitable pup may turn into a quiet, reserved dog. A well socialized Bernedoodle may even try to avoid other animals or rambunctious children at this stage. During this time, respect its reservations towards others and try not to put it in a position it would rather not be in. Old dogs may be more easily annoyed by young children, which can cause them to snap. Limit the amount of time your crotchety old dog interacts with children and other dogs, and always give it a quiet space to escape to.

This is also not a great time for any major life changes. Moving to a new home, changing the feeding and exercise schedule, or having new pets or people in the home may not be welcomed by an aging dog. Of course, you can't always put your life on hold because of an old dog, but keep this in mind when making decisions that will affect your dog's life.

While your dog is going through some changes during this stage, it doesn't mean that its life is over. If you keep your dog in good health, you'll still have plenty of time with your Bernedoodle. Note changes, and if anything seems abnormal, discuss these changes with your vet.

Grooming a Senior Dog

Just because your Bernedoodle is old doesn't mean that it should not be groomed. When grooming an older dog, one must take the dog's comfort into account. Senior dogs have more aches and pains than a younger dog, so even a light touch in the wrong place can cause a lot of distress. Some older dogs can be cranky around others, so for everyone's safety, grooming should be gentle and simple.

Your aging Bernedoodle's safety is especially important at this stage in its life. Baths should have non-slip surfaces because a fall could cause a lot of damage to already damaged joints. Any grooming surfaces should also be non-slip and even padded for extra comfort. A groomer may want to work with the dog in a comfortable prone position because standing for too long may be difficult for some dogs. When bringing your old dog to a groomer, ask them about their experience with working with senior dogs. They should be able to tell you how they accommodate dogs in this stage of life.

As far as home grooming goes, your Bernedoodle still needs to be brushed regularly. If its fur becomes too matted, it will have to be professionally de-matted or shaved. Removing large mats can be painful for a sensitive dog, and shaving may cause it to become too cold. Keeping up with regular brushing prevents these issues in the first place. You may find that your dog will not stay still for as long or cannot hold a certain position for as long as it takes to brush it. In this case, you may want to brush it in sections, allowing for a break between each brushing.

Photo Courtesy of Gina StVrain

Continue to trim its nails, never leaving them long enough to press into the ground. The pressure from the nails hitting a hard surface can cause a lot of pain in sore foot joints. You may find that it doesn't enjoy having its nails clipped as much as usual, but it will save it a lot of pain.

Teeth should also be brushed because gum disease is often apparent in older dogs. However, if you've kept up the habit of brushing the teeth its entire life, the teeth shouldn't be in too bad of shape. Gum disease will cause the gums to be more sensitive and bleed more easily, so use a soft brush and a gentle hand. Good oral hygiene is one thing that can extend the life of your dog.

If your aging dog has trouble keeping its bottom clean after using the bathroom, talk to your groomer about cutting the hair in a way that can help it stay clean. Not only will it keep your home clean and sanitary, but it will also help reduce the risk of your dog becoming infected or matted around those areas. At home, give it a quick wipe with a washcloth or disposable wipe to keep it clean.

Nutrition

One of the biggest concerns when it comes to a senior dog's nutrition is the amount of calories it's ingesting. If a young, active dog eats two cups of food a day to maintain a healthy weight, a senior dog requires less. Younger dogs burn many more calories because they are able to run and play more. An older dog may spend more time sleeping and walking at a moderate pace. If it continues to eat the same amount as it did as a young dog, it will gain weight.

Excessive weight gain is not good for any dog, but it can be especially hard on old dogs. Their joints have worn down more, just from daily use for many years. Their internal organs may also not work at full capacity, so a thick layer of fat causes more strain. For this reason, food levels need to be adjusted to account for a less active lifestyle. Check your dog's weight regularly and slowly adjust food intake accordingly. Suddenly cutting back on food might confuse your dog and might leave it feeling hungry if it's used to getting the same amount every day. If your overweight dog complains, don't give in to the whining and begging—it will get used to the change eventually.

There are even dog foods on the market to address the nutritional needs of senior dogs. These come with fewer calories to prevent weight gain, and extra fiber for regular digestion. These special foods may also contain nutrients for joint health. However, a large dog's food will already contain most of these ingredients. While senior dog formulas can provide the right nutrition for your aging dog, they aren't absolutely necessary unless your dog has special dietary needs. Give the correct portion for meals, and it will help keep extra weight from piling on.

Because dog treats are filled with calories, you may want to opt for fruits and vegetables. These are low in calories and contain lots of vitamins and minerals that dogs of all ages need. Older dogs also tend to get dehydrated more easily, so they should always have a bowl full of clean water to encourage them to drink more.

Sometimes, a dog chooses not to eat as much as it normally would. Sometimes this is due to disease and needs treatment from a vet. But if its teeth are sore, it may not want to eat large, crunchy kibble. For a dog who won't eat its dry food, try to add something to soften it up. A few spoonfuls of canned food or some soup broth can make the food softer and more enticing to eat. Even a bit of warm water will soften the food and release yummy aromas. Because soft foods stick to teeth easier than crunchy foods, remember to brush on a regular basis.

Exercise

When it comes to exercise, your dog may not be able to do as much as it used to. However, this doesn't mean that it should just lounge around the home all day. As your dog changes, its exercise routine should change too. Keep a close eye on your dog so you can pick up cues of when it is tired or in pain.

High intensity games like fetch or Frisbee might be too much for an older dog. The running and jumping can put a lot of stress on its legs. Still, even old dogs love to play and will want to continue playing as long as you're willing. When playing these kinds of games, play for shorter amounts of time. While your young dog would want to play fetch for longer than thirty minutes, ten minutes of play might be more appropriate for a senior dog.

The same goes for going on walks. Getting out of the house and going on a walk is great for a senior dog because even old dogs can get bored. However, if you notice that your dog gets tired after a half hour of walking, adjust your distance so you can make it home before your dog is too wiped out. You may even decide to walk laps around the block; this way your dog has the chance to stop for a drink of water or a rest in between.

Most importantly, don't push your dog to do any more than it's capable of. Don't try to get your dog into distance running shape at the age of nine. The truth is, if it isn't running willingly, then it's probably past that stage in its life. An injury from overexerting itself can keep it sidelined for a while, which could lead to boredom or weight gain.

Mental Stimulation

As dogs age, their brains don't always function as well as they used to. Some dogs can even develop dementia in advanced age. Along with physical exercise, dogs need mental exercise.

If your dog is up to it, continue teaching new commands. Bernedoodles love to learn and should have the opportunity to learn new commands for the duration of their life. If you've taught your dog every trick in the book, work on naming objects. Having it collect objects by name is a fun, non-strenuous way to play with your dog. Depending on your dog's sight and hearing, you can adapt commands to fit its impairments. If your old dog still has its vision, but its hearing is gone, try teaching commands with hand signals.

Puzzle toys are also great for older dogs. There are toys that can be filled with treats that require your dog to push it around or move the object in a certain way to get it to release the yummy snack. Not only does it keep your dog's mind sharp, but it keeps it happy and entertained.

Some senior dogs like to socialize with others, while some don't. If your dog is still happy to be around other people and pets, arrange play dates. While a dog park can seem like an open invitation to be ambushed by people and dogs of all ages, a controlled setting might be a better pace for your dog. That way, you can choose more laid-back dogs to visit your Bernedoodle.

Common Old-Age Ailments

Unfortunately, your Bernedoodle's health will slowly decline as it lives out its remaining years. While this can be sad to see, it's a normal part of life. Most symptoms can be dealt with as they show up to improve your dog's quality of life.

In addition to sore, stiff joints, and decreased mental sharpness, senior dogs will begin to show other symptoms of poor health. It's very common for old dogs to develop various types of cancers, urinary tract infections, and kidney, heart, and liver disease. If you're concerned about your dog developing any of these conditions, some owners increase the frequency of their vet checkups from once a year to twice a year. This can help the vet catch problems that you might not.

Older dogs also have a tougher time healing from minor injuries and illnesses that a younger dog would bounce right back from. Internal and external parasites can put a large strain on an older dog's body, so stay vigilant with your parasite prevention and care. Small cuts and scratches may become infected more easily, so do your best to keep your dog's injuries clean.

In general, the slow decline of its health might make it feel uncomfortable. Make sure it never gets too hot or too cold, and give it soft, padded areas to hang out in. When relaxing with your dog, you may even massage its sore muscles in addition to petting it.

Photo Courtesy of Alicia Marshall
"Highfalutin Furry Babies Bernedoodles"

Photo Courtesy of Maggie Box
www.angelviewdoodles.com

Sadly, there may come a time where your dog's quality of life is poor enough to cause suffering. No one wants to see their dog go, but you may want to have a plan with your vet if its health takes a turn for the worst. Signs of this include lameness, incontinence, and depression. It's tough to do, but you have to think about what's best for your dog.

If your Bernedoodle has lived a healthy life full of good nutrition, exercise, and proper hygiene, its senior stage should be a breeze. Good care throughout a dog's life can improve its quality of life, even in old age. While your dog may change, it'll still be a joy to be around. Give it a little extra care, and it will give you extra love in return.

Bernedoodles make fantastic companions for different types of homes. Whether you live alone or have a full house, your Bernedoodle will be a friend for life. These intelligent dogs are fun and absolutely adorable. Raising a dog from the puppy stage or adopting an adult dog can make for challenging work, but these loving dogs make it all worth it. It is a joy to bring a Bernedoodle into your home because with proper care, it will dedicate its life to making its owners happy.

Made in the USA
Columbia, SC
03 April 2021